SECULARISM
AND
INDIAN PRESS

SECULARISM AND INDIAN PRESS

C.S.H.N. MURTHY
Assistant Professor
in Mass Communication (Reader)
Amity School of Communication
AMITY UNIVERSITY LUCKNOW/NOIDA
(U.P.)

KANISHKA PUBLISHERS, DISTRIBUTORS
NEW DELHI-110 002

KANISHKA PUBLISHERS, DISTRIBUTORS
4697/5-21 A, Ansari Road, Daryaganj
New Delhi-110 002
Phones : 2327 0497, 2328 8285
Fax : 011-2328 8285
e-mail: kanishka_publishing@yahoo.co.in

First Published 2007

ISBN 978-81-7391-992-3

PRINTED IN INDIA

Published by Madan Sachdeva for Kanishka Publishers, Distributors, 4697/5-21A, Ansari Road, Daryaganj, New Delhi-110 002, Typeset by Sunshine Graphics, Delhi, and Printed at Nice Printing Press, Delhi.

Preface

I chose this subject for my M.Phil dissertation, as the prevailing situation in India that time was quite agitating and consequently inspiring. The nation turned into an inferno, firstly due to V.P. Singh's overambitious plan to woo Minorities and Backward classes by implementing controversial report of B.P. Mandal Commission, followed by Rath Yatra carried out by L.K. Advani, who claimed that it would subdue the communal and caste flames roused by V.P. Singh, and finally the events leading to the construction of Ram Temple by BJP, VHP, RSS and Bajrang Dal combine, which led to the eventual demolition of Babri Masjid itself. The subject was indeed thought provoking and raised many questions as to the true import of *secularism* besides the critical role played by the media which instead of enacting the role of a *watchdog, besides agenda setting and gate keeping,* helped accentuate the division among people and political parties further on this sensitive and delicate issue.

The situation is no different even today nearly 14 years after the demolition of Babri Masjid. Recent controversial statements of Mr. Rahul Gandhi, a budding leader from Nehru-Gandhi family in the UP Road Show (in connection with ongoing election campaign) on the demolition of Babri Masjid only proved the fact that political leaders are not willing to learn any lesson from the past. What more surprises a common man is self-proclamation by each party that it is *secular* and that only BJP and Shiv Sena are "non-secular". In reality there is no *secular* party or professing of 'secularism' anywhere even in the Media. Today, religion and caste have become launch pads for political parties to make or unmake the governments. No other issue than caste or religion will tilt the fortunes of any political party to climb the ladder of political power. As such they do not hesitate to divide the society on these lines more and more till people wake up to the grand political fraud wrought on the nation.

What stares into our face 60 years after independence is — What is "secularism" at all? Who defines it? Political Parties, Parliament or Judiciary? Even media conveniently and comfortably skirts the issue and enters into deep slumber on this issue. But, the term 'secularism' is a constant refrain one hears or reads from political parties or print/electronic media.

The present study exposes the pretensions of media, besides the known game of fraud that all political parties often perpetrate from time to time in a bid to capture power. For instance so-called *secular* Devea Gouda's Janata Dal is happily hand in glove with the BJP in the Karnataka. What happened to Deve Gouda's all time rhetoric to keep the BJP away from power by realignments and polarizations since the time of his being the Prime Minister which did not last long, though. What happened to BJP-Akali Dal in Punjab? They returned to power dumping the so-called *secular* Congress which portrays itself as messiah of minorities? Are not Sikhs minorities? Why did they dump the Congress and embrace a non-secular BJP-Akali Dal? Why the perception of electorate and that of political parties do not coincide with the definition of *secularism*? Why BJP is being voted back to power again and again in Madhya Pradesh, Rajasthan, Gujarat, Uttaranchal and Karnataka? Are the people here rejecting the so-called *secular* parties or accepting BJP as *true secular* party.

If one deeply pays attention to the nuanced verdict of the peoples across the country, it would be clear that the electorate stopped buying the definitions offered by the intellectuals/ideologues of various political parties to *secularism*. Hence the arguments of Leftists that they are supporting the Congress at the Centre only to keep BJP out of power is nothing but a gross distortion and opportunistic talk, which flies in the face of reason. It is all a fraud which this nation is continuously facing and suffering from. Thus, the study has more relevance even today as much as two decades back. I leave it to the fellow journalists, intellectuals, and students of journalism to read this once and arrive at exactly what uncertainties are plaguing the nation and where we are all heading towards in the next decade?

I take this as an opportunity to place on record my deep sense of gratitude and indebtedness to Professor P.L. Visweswara Rao, Department of Communication and Journalism, for his constant encouragement and support. I also thank, Dr. V. Shyam Sunder,

Head Department, Dr. K. Stevenson, Dr. K. Nageswar, Dr.Narendra, Dr. Balaswamy and Dr. Padmaja Shaw and other faculty members of the Department for their continued help and highly useful suggestions that enabled completion of this research work.

It is my pleasure to keep on record my special thanks to Dr. G. Nagamallika, Associate Professor, Manipal Institute of Mass Communication, Manipal University, Udipi for her kind suggestions during the Seminar which qualitatively and analytically helped improving the thesis.

I also thank the Indian Express and The Hindu Newspaper Managements for allowing their Editorials, Edit Page, Non-Edit Page Articles and Sunday Magazine articles to be used for a critical analysis in this study. I also place on record my deep sense of gratitude to The Hindu for permitting me to use the pictures of Shankar Chakravarthy, Subir Roy and V. Sudershan who captured the exciting moments of the demolition of the Babri Masjid, that changed the course of the Indian history irrevocably.

I also thank my two lovely children Malavika Vagdevi and Subrahmanya Chandrahas for their standing by my side during the stress and strain and extending emotional support to overcome all the hurdles and complete this work belated though.

C.S.H.N. MURTHY

Contents

Preface v

1. **What is True Secularism ?** **1**
   - Introduction
   - Political Polarizations
   - Objectives of Study
   - Chapterization

2. **Methodology of Study** **10**
   - Statement of the Problem
   - Methodology and Discourse: Content Analysis
   - Operational Design
   - Sampling of the Content
   - Tests Reliability and Validity: Inter Reliability of Coding
   - Graphical and Statistical Data for Analysis
   - Justification of the Sample: *The Indian Express* and *The Hindu*

3. **Secularism: Thematic Analysis of Theoretical Issues** **25**
   - Literary Definition
   - Sociological and Revolutionary Origins
   - Secularization and Secularism
   - Spiritual and Philosophical Interpretation
   - Secular Characters of India as on the August 15, 1947
   - Constitutional
   - Deterimining Objectivity in Interpretations

4. **Ayodhya Ram Janmabhoomi-Babri Masjid Movement: A Focal Point** **49**

5. **Portrayal of Secularism : Unit and Item Analysis of Indian Express** **55**
- Analysis of the Editorials
- Analysis of the Edit Page Articles
- Analysis of Non-Edit Page Articles Written by Politicans and Intellectuals
- Analysis of Articles of Sunday Magazine

6. **Portrayal of Secularism in the Media: Unit Analysis and Item Anlysis of The Hindu** **102**
- Analysis of the Editorials of *The Hindu*
- Statistical Analysis
- Analysis of the Edit Page Articles in *The Hindu*
- Analysis of Non-Edit Page Articles
- Analysis of Sunday Magazine Articles
- Analysis of Interviews

7. **Discussion and Conclusions** **138**
- Treatment of Editorials of *Indian Express* and *The Hindu*
- Treatment of Edit Page Articles *Indian Express* and *The Hindu*
- Treatment of Non-Edit Page Articles in *Indian Express* and *The Hindu*
- Treatment of Articles Published in Sunday Magazine of *Indian Express* and *The Hindu*
- Interviews Published in *The Hindu*
- Conclusions
- Suggestions for Further Study

Bibliography **150**

Index **159**

1
What is True Secularism?

Introduction

It is a universal reality that Media and Politics go together. They are mutually interdependent for the rapid growth and spread. Before the onset of electronic media, the print medium in its variety of forms—handouts, pamphlets, brochures, letters, posters, tabloids, daily newspapers, weeklies and monthlies—contributed to the richness and to the diversity of thinking in the realm of Politics across the globe (Chalapati Rau: 200 Years of the Indian Press, Vidura, Feb., 1980; J.V.Vilanilam: Mass Communication in India, 2005, p. 48). Soon the world recognized that no political organization, whether autocratic or democratic, could survive without a compatible medium of communication (at least relevant to its own ethos). Whereas democratic societies recognized the Media as a value addition to the very survival of Democracy, the other administrative dispensations too felt the need to communicate with its subjects through Media, even if it were to be under controlled conditions arising out of dictatorial and Machiavellian governance.

As Media occupied the center stage in public life, its role as an effective medium of communication began to evolve over years. In certain democratic societies Media enjoyed special status under constitutional provisions (e.g. USA). In India the Media came to be regarded as fourth estate and enjoyed a lot of respect and freedom, though its degree of freedom did not go beyond the freedom of speech guaranteed under article 19 (1b) of Indian Constitution (Durga Das Basu, pp. 26-29: 1993). Like anywhere in the world, Media in India also began to evolve along the sidelines of the growth of freedom struggle. Many of our freedom fighters of 18th and 19th centuries were either founders of various forms of Media for political propaganda and spread of their messages or ideas or journalists of eminence during freedom struggle. As such the role of Media in a democratic set-up like ours could hardly be overemphasized. Simply put, the Indian press is repute for its churning out a lot of information, which includes that of nuisance value, on the basis of day to day political developments right from Gram Panchayat to Parliament (Goswami, N: A carnival of clones, Indian Express, New Delhi, July 24, 1994).

Yet, when it came to research in assessing the role of Media, as mass communicator, a few scientific studies have by far been documented as to how Media performed its role with regard to the issues of public concern. There is still far more left to be desired. Efficacy, objectivity and impact—are three primary concerns of Media role in any democratic society, where media growth and development seemed to be linked to the Politics directly.

Though Media always contributed to enrichment of information through an open discussion, enlightenment and entertainment—the primary objectives—sometimes for a variety of reasons media would indulge in an unprecedented hype, may be, as part of its *agenda setting*. Sometimes it may deliberately avoid performing proper gate-keeping for various reasons. Whereas political organizations keep changing their priorities based on the contemporary social developments obtaining from time to time, Media had no option but keep pace with such fast changing scenario. In the process, Media and the Politics seemed to be vying with each other. Certain times, Media get aligned with certain political hues and serve to be effective instruments of communication of political ideologies. Newspapers like Indian Express was known for spearheading agitation against emergency and press censorship imposed by Mrs. Indira Gandhi in late 1977 under the leadership of late Jayaprakash Narayan. In the process, the content reflected in the Media may play a pivotal role in tilting the scales in favour of a political party or a combination. Especially in third world democratic countries like India, this played a very vital role for the survival of a political party.

Against the backdrop, the present study intends to critically evaluate the Portrayal of Secularism, limited though, in the mainstream press in the aftermath of the demolition of Babri Masjid at Ayodhya on December 6, 1992. Never in the history of India perhaps is there so much crescendo of discussion and controversy centered around a word *secularism*, which is a much sought after term, embedded with the potential of an atom bomb, for all the politicians, both the old and new alike, to use it for their self-serving political ends, as it is witnessed now in the last decade of 20th Century (Durga Das Basu, p. 29, 1993). Though the word *secularism* first appears in the preamble of Indian Constitution as an imported doctrine of defining the State (as contrasted with the Church), following the 42nd amendment to the Constitution in 1976 during the Prime Ministership of Indira Gandhi, as an imposition on the rich values, cultures and traditions of India for which it is known for thousands of years, the repercussions of such an inclusion began telling upon the collective conscience of the country more strikingly in the early nineties, mainly due to the aggressive politics pursued by several political parties exploiting the word *minorities vis a vis secularism* for their vested interests. In the his famous book, An Introduction to Constitution of India, under the chapter of the Philosophy of the Constitution, Durga Das Basu (1993) highlighted this as follows:

> It must be pointed out, in this context, that both *socialism* and *secularism* are vague words, and in the absence of any explanation of these words in the Constitution, such vagueness is liable to be capitalized by the interested political groups and to create confusion in the minds of masses of the republic to instruct whom is one of the objects of the Preamble. The Janata Party sought to offer such explanation, by Amending Article 366 of the Constitution by the 45th Amendment Bill, 1976, which, however, was thwarted by the Congress opposition in the Rajya Sabha. In the absence of such explanation, it would remain a matter of controversy whether the object of *socialism* under the Indian Constitution simply means 'freedom from exploitation' or *State Socialism* or even Marxism.
>
> Similarly, *secularism* might be used as an instrument of unrestrained communalism or bigotry or even anti-religionism, as distinguished from 'equal respect for all religions'. Instead of these words serving to elucidate the

articles of the Constitution, the meaning of these words shall have to be gathered from the operative provisions, which, in legal interpretation, cannot be controlled by the Preamble.

It does not mean that these repercussions were not there before. Indeed the nation was experiencing these repercussions time and again since January 26, 1950 itself, when the Constitution first came into force, against the backdrop of unprecedented bloodshed and mayhem, arising out of the partition as a result of a two nation theory, which gave Pakistan an edge to establish itself as a theocratic State governed by Islamic law. By trying to proclaim India as a *Secular* state, according to 42nd amendment, the Constitution of India specifically ruled out any possibility to give room for any specific religion the status of the 'established Church' as some constitutions and some countries {Pakistan (Islam), Bangladesh (Islam), Srilanka (Buddhism) and Burma (Buddhism)} claimed to follow and blindly believed that it would strengthen India rather than weaken it. But, it was hard to believe that this very idea was quite conveniently exploited later on as a political strategy by the Congress, headed by the Prime Minister Indira Gandhi, to appease religious minorities especially Muslims and willy-nilly gave rise, in the course of post-independent era, to a number of conflicts and controversies as the people began experiencing its polity.

The reason for such thinking is obviously not unfounded in the light of the timing the amendment was carried out. It was the 'emergency' period, which gave the people of India the first taste of draconian administration and rule since independent India.

Although, one were to believe, that this was not the same case with the constitutional founders who while voting the constitution on November 26, 1949, in the course of time it led to establishing on the political landscape—a hitherto clandestine political link between the two controversial constitutional words—*secularism* and *minorities*—both of which willy-nilly sowed seeds for the birth of many political parties and leaders that India witnessed by the turn of 20th century. The unholy nexus, thus founded between the two words—*secularism* and *minorities* by some political opportunists to enhance their political fortunes, has changed over decades the political alignments and realignments of the country as a whole. This has witnessed a concomitant polarization of socio, economic and cultural forces too from the grass roots level to the top level both in the government as well as non-government sectors. The following is a short-list of such polarizations for a brief overview of how opportunistic alignments and realignments made all the difference to India with the *secularism* and *minorities* at the center of the political stage.

Political Polarizations

A political polarization may be defined as *ideologically opposite political parties grouping themselves or forging an alliance to form into one political major front with a singular agenda to oppose and defeat one larger political entity in the elections.* Therefore mostly they are temporary alliances and are likely to fall or split again based on their original ideological bases or differences (Niraja Gopal Jayal: Introduction in Democracy in India, pp. 1-49, 2001).

1. There were first ever polarizations against the Congress' rule for over 30 years in 1975 when the Janata Party, under the vibrant collective leadership of Jayaprakash Narayan, Morarji Desai, Vajpayee and George Fernandes, was catapulted to power in 1977(1947-77 witnessed the rule Jawaharlal Nehru ('47-'64:17 years), Lal Bahadur Shastry ('64-'66:2 years) and Indira Gandhi ('66 to'77: 11 years). It was the first ever non-Congress government at the Center in the post independent era.
2. In the first ever polarizations, which took place between 1975-77 (during the rule of emergency and the period preceding it), it was Congress, draconian misrule that brought all the political forces, which inter alia included such sworn political rivals like Jana Sangh and Communists too, together the apparent contradictions among the ideologies of these political forces notwithstanding.
3. It proved to be a turning point in the history of post-independent India as Congress was for the first time reduced to a mere opposition having 147 MPs (with CM Stephen as the leader of the Congress in the opposition while Indira Gandhi lost her election at the hustings) in the Lok Sabha with the Janata Party comprising a hotch-potch of all other political parties as mentioned earlier forming a Government at the Center.
4. The Jana Sangh, it should be noted, which was the constituent of the then Janata Party, was accusing both the

Congress and the Left parties of having pursued the politics of *pseudo-secularism* and *appeasement of minorities* in those crucial elections that changed the course of Indian history too. At this time none of the constituents of the Janata Party found the Jana Sangh as a communal party or for a moment, for our own logical understanding to take this way forward to draw some important analyses in the subsequent chapters, it could also be interpreted that they might have ignored the communal character of Jana Sangh as the sole aim of all the political parties that time was to defeat the Congress.

5. But within two years of the Janata rule (which was considered the best rule in the post-independent era by the people) the same political parties, which ignored the communal character of Jana Sangh earlier as frivolous, took cognizance of the same and decided to vertically split the Janata Party, reducing Morarji Desai's Government to minority in a matter of 3 days. The first person to quit the Janata Party accusing its formation as an unholy and opportunistic nexus with communal elements such as Jana Sangh was George Fernandes preceded by Raj Narayan and others. Inevitably this defection or split led to the fall of Morarji Government and Choudhury Charan Singh became the Prime Minister with the support of the Congress group led by C.M. Stephen from outside only to last for 45 days after which Lok Sabha was dissolved and nationwide snap poll was called for by the then President N. Sanjeeva Reddy. Ultimately, Choudhury Charan Singh remained in the history as the only Prime Minister who never faced the Parliament.

All the above points, if subjected to a test of logic, bring into sharp focus several important questions concerning the hue and cry raised about *secularism* or *secular character* of both the political parties and that of India, and leaves behind a legacy of enormous conflicts and confusion by way of plenty of jargon and vocabulary with a bewildering variety of definitions and interpretations stemming out.

Further, it gives us insights how the *core ideas of secularism* played a key role in the change and transition of political power both at the Center and the State by giving rise to different combinations of political governance from time to time. In the end, what (the term *secularism*) needs to be determining the simple nature and the character of the State, in accordance with the spirit of the Constitution, has come to indulge in a power play, surpassing all other important factors like economy, agriculture, eradication of poverty and illiteracy, gender equality and gender development, far beyond the imagination of all. Precisely put, it is *secularism* and *power play* than anything else that steered the course of the Indian Democracy in the last one decade of Indian political governance.

Against the backdrop, the following questions, therefore, need to be addressed to in order for an analysis and understanding (in terms of methodology as explained later in the methodology chapter) the media role to determine what went wrong with the Indian *secularism*, whether it has in reality different connotations and facets to meet the opportune alliances and equations, what are the different factors or agents (socio-economic and political) responsible for the present confusion about the nature of *secularism* pursued in India by various political groups and to assess the role of media insofar as contributing to the above phenomena.

The present study being interdisciplinary in nature, involving two powerful social organizations – Media and Politics – whatever was discussed in the foregoing would be studied in depth to meet the following objectives with an emphasis how media coverage, which was vital for the growth and development of politics, had contributed to the popular understanding of the interplay between *secularism* and *politics*, with all its positive as well as negative consequences threatening the integrity of the nation and peaceful co-existence of populace.

Objectives of the Study

1. What is *secularism* according to Indian Constitution vis-a-vis Western perspective and to identify, differentiate and determine to what extent the *concepts* and *definitions* offered to *secularism* by political parties and journalists in the media are relevant to Indian context and does vagueness exist over the Indian approach to *secularism*?
2. Do the words *secularism* and *minorities*, spelt out variously in the Media by all political groups, are ipso facto mutually so inter-related and interdependent as to help exploit the communal feelings of the Hindus and the Muslims?

3. To probe and assess how the term *secularism* is used as a political ploy or design in the Media, against the backdrop of political ideologies, by different political parties to catapult their political ambitions and fortunes by seeking to interlink *secularism* and *minorities* to flare up the communal passions across the country?
4. Who would decide the communal character of a political party and how it was achieved through its discourse and portrayal in the Media and should Media certify that a particular political party is above communal politics and has a correct view of *secularism*?
5. To what extent this polarization of politics on communal or secular lines had affected the social strata including the Indian press?

The scope of this dissertation therefore is limited to analyzing the above questions purely from the framework of Content Analysis with categories and parameters constructed and fitted into its frame as relevant to Indian context and made applicable Indian Express and The Hindu, especially with reference to the articles of editors, politicians, journalists, intellectuals, ideologues and authors in the aftermath of the demolition of Babri Masjid on the fateful day of December 6, 1992, against a historical and constitutional canvass and to ascertain how far Media institutions had objectively portrayed the *secularism*.

Chapterization

In the process the dissertation is divided into the following Chapters:

Chapter 1 deals with the background, which necessitated the present study and details the objectives of the study. It also makes clear the subject is inter-disciplinary in nature dealing with the socio-political dimension of Indian polity. Thus one finds tinges of Political Science in it though limited in theory and its application.

Chapter 2 deals with *Statement of Problem and Methodology* expounding the theoretical background of the chosen methodology and finally how the actual methodology had been worked out to fit into the chosen specific methodology.

Chapter 3 deals with all the theoretical facets of *Secularism* around which the present study revolves. It dealt with briefly the literary, sociological, philosophical and spiritual, besides constitutional definitions and interpretations of *secularism* as understood in the West and in India and attempts to bring to the fore the imbalances in the definition and interpretations that led to the present crisis.

Chapter 4 deals with the significance of Ayodhya Ram Janmabhoomi and Babri Masjid imbroglio in-so-far turning out to be a rallying point in the post-independent era arousing a deep interest among populace in the subject *secularism* that is being pretended to be followed by all political parties claiming themselves *secular.* It also endeavours to show how shortsighted political pursuits by the vested interests of the political parties brought deep sense of alienation both among Hindus and Muslims.

Chapter 5 deals with the *Media Analysis* of the universe of the sample—Indian Express—with reference to Editorials, Edit Page Articles, and Non-Edit Page Contributions by Politicians, Ideologues, Journalists and Intellectuals.

Chapter 6 deals with the *Media Analysis* of the universe of the sample—The Hindu—with reference to Editorials, Edit Page Articles, and Non-Edit Page Contributions by Politicians, Ideologues, Journalists and Intellectuals.

Chapter 7 deals with the *Discussion and Conclusions* of the Media Analyses done in Chapters 5 and 6.

In the end an exhaustive *Bibliography* was furnished.

All through the dissertation the term *secularism* and *secular* are kept in inverted commas to suggest vagueness shrouding the precise meaning as relevant and applicable to India and acceptable to all political hues.

2

Methodology of Study

Statement of the Problem

It is hypothesized that in a multi-cultural and pluralistic setting like India, lack of precision as to the definition and scope of the words like *secularism* and *minority* in the Constitution has offered an ample leverage to the over -ambitious and enthusiastic political groups to exploit the sensitivities of the populace through Media and this in turn has led to the opportunistic polarizations, alignments and realignments among the political forces triggering off a similar polarization across all the sections including the Press which is supposed to play an *objective* and *constructive* role. It is also hypothesized that due to the failure of the media institutions to play a dispassionate, constructive and objective role, the country witnessed a terrible and unprecedented political crisis, turmoil and anarchy in the last one decade (1990-96) which has the prospects of continuing the crisis further into the next decade of the new millennium and polarizing the media itself between the so-called *secular* and *communal* political groups.

Methodology and Discourse: Content Analysis

Type of Research: Descriptive, Analytical and Nominal

The study has been *Descriptive, Analytical* and *Nominal* carried out by subjecting the content of the articles of various authors, including those appeared in the Edit pages and the Editorials of the mainstream press, to a test of critical and rigorous analysis to determine:

(*i*) whether the arguments advanced, terminology (specific

words) used and the description given (with slant/without slant) in the Content of the articles are in keeping with the discourse on Secularism (Chapter III—Thematic Analysis and Theoretical issues) and in conformity thereof;

(ii) to identify and highlight specific logics and statements put forward in the selected articles by the authors to show how the media and the journalists, authors became vulnerable to depicting facts in slant/distortion and indulged in the politicization of 'secularism'; and

(iii) how they (the authors and media) struggled hard to align themselves with specific political schools of thought throwing the Ethics of Media to the winds pitching conflicting and anti-secular feelings against the secular foundations of the country and Constitution.

The study is therefore predominantly semi-quantitative and qualitative. Stress is not placed on quantification of the data only to subject it to the rigorous statistical tools/tests such as Chi-square test or T- Test I and II or ANOVA, etc. Stress is placed on the 'manifest content' as it conveyed the messages through Editorials, Edit page articles, etc. The reason for such a decision is necessitated by the fact that there is a complexity in the content to be analyzed in these articles and therefore quanitification of the content in the form of scales such as Lickert scales etc. may not be relevant as in the case of opinion surveys.

No Previously Documented Study or Research in this Area

Further, the researcher has found no previously documented work in this area of the subject. In fact, the researcher perused a number of latest available Theses/Dissertaions done on the Content Analysis in India and most of them are not interdisciplinary such as this one. Secondly, most of the works done using Content Analysis with Quantificiation of data were chosen in such a way that they exactly fitted into the Western models of Content Analysis as prescribed by Bereleson (1952) or Gudio Stempel (1989) or Wimmer and Dominik (2003). The researcher also found that the topics chosen for following the Western models of content analysis are typical in nature and look like tailor made or cut-slices.

For instance the topic "Developmental News Coverage in the Indian Press: An analysis of Four Dailies" done by D.V.R. Murthy

(Media Asia: Vol 27, No. 1: 2000, pp. 24-29, 53) well fit into the Western model of Content Analysis due to the possibility of quantifying enormous data in inches and centimeters. But, in terms of relevance, one wonders how Development News Coverage could be quantified and analysed based on the Mainstream Press content as they (Development Journals and Mainstream Press) are mutually opposite entities by character and definition per se (Shelton Gunaratne: "Media Subservience and Developmental Journalism" Communications and Development Review, Vol. 2, No. 2, pp. 3-7). Such an approach will not permit chosing variety of topics which, like the current topic, have greater social relevance to Indian Culture and Polity. Many topics may not simply fit into the quantification as relevant to Content Analysis.

On the contrary G. Nagamallika had done "The Coverage of Communal Riots in Hyderabad" (Ph.D. Thesis: University of Hyderabad, 2002) wherein she had approached the subject totally from the Qualitative Analysis using the hybrid methodologies adopted by J.B. Thompson and Straus, not any particular one methodology in full.

As such this researcher believes that the Content Analysis in Indian Context will have to be with its own parameters arising from Indian cultural contexts as operational design though the broad framework of the Western model can yet be used. Against the backdrop the researcher felt that he could more focus on the qualitiative part and use quantitative analysis in a limited way to back the qualitiative interpretation. Guido Stempel III (1989) also supports this view.

Broad Framework of Content Analysis: A Short Discourse (Berelson, Guido Stempel III and Wimmer and Dominick)

The place of content analysis in communication research is indicated by the following paradigm for communication research:

WHO says WHAT to WHOM with WHAT EFFECT?

"It is evident that communication research has not dealt equally with all four parts of this paradigm, but we did not introduce it here to make that point. Rather, we bring it up to suggest that communication research can realize its full potential only if it can relate content to communicator, audience and effects" argued Guido

H. Stempel III (pp. 119-131; 1989) while dealing with the description of Berelson methodology (p. 18; 1952) which provided a classic definition of content analysis twenty-five years ago:

> Content analysis is a research technique for the objective, systematic and quantitative description of the manifest communication.

According to Berelson the key to understanding content analysis and performing it competently lies in understanding the meaning of *objective, systematic, quantitative and manifest content (Berelson, 1952).* At the heart of any content analysis is the category system used to classify media content (Wimmer and Dominick, 2003). The precise make up of the system, of course varies with the topic under study, says Wiimer and Dominick. Berelson (1952) pointed out, "Particular studies have been productive to the extent that the categories were clearly formulated and well adapted to the problem and the content."

Walizer and Wienir (1978) defined it as any systematic procedure devised to examine the content of recorded information (Wimmer, R.D. and Dominick, J.R.: Mass Media Research: An Introduction, p. 140, 2003). Kerlinger's (2000) definition is fairly typical: Content is a method of studying and analyzing communication in a systematic, objective and quantitative manner for the purpose of measuring variables, (Wimmer, R.D. and Dominick J.R., 2003).

Berelson defined the above four terms as follows:

Objective

It begins with the opposite of subjective or impressionistic. Objectivity is achieved by having the categories of analysis defined so precisely that different persons can apply them to the same content and get the same results. If content analysis were subjective instead of objective, each person would have his own content analysis. That it is objective means that the results depend upon the procedure and not the analyst.

Systematic

Means that at first a set procedure is applied in the same way to all the content being analyzed. Second, it means that categories are set- up so that all relevant content is analyzed. Finally, it means that the analyses are designed to secure data relevant to a research question.

Quantitative

Means simply recording of numerical values or the frequencies with which the various defined types of content occur.

Manifest Content

Means the apparent content, which means that content, must be coded as it appears rather than as the content analyst feels it is intended.

Stempel III (1989) argues further that there has been little quarrel with the first two points in Berelson's definition but there are different views as to the quantitative and manifest content. The counter argument against Berelson's quantitative one was that it should be qualitative as far as content analysis is concerned. It was also found that some researchers confused indicators related to systematic organization for quantitative measurement, pointed out Stempel III (1989). Similarly, the concept of manifest content has been criticized by those who balk at dealing with the apparent content when they are certain that the intent of the communicator is otherwise and are equally certain that they know what it is. This viewpoint has a certain appeal, says Stempel III, but the question is whether objectivity could be maintained if manifest content is abandoned. The content analyst at this point of course injects a subjective interpretation—whether one feels that it is an obviously correct interpretation and whether one will see the situation in the same terms. The concern however probably could be dealt with more effectively by interpreting the results accordingly than by giving up on manifest content, argues Stempel III (1989).

Further Stempel III (1989) suggested four methodological problems for content analysis in communication research.

(i) *Selection of the Unit Analysis*: This pertains to the kind of content we are going to consider whether they are words, statements, sentences, paragraphs or entire articles. Where the analysis is related to the statements or opinions expressed, it is suggested to take the whole articles into consideration. If the kind of content could be set on a range of parameters like favorable, unfavorable and neutral, it is ideal to follow this content as Unit. It all depends primarily on what information is required for the purpose of the study.

(ii) *Category Construction*: There are two systems suggested under this: (1) Laswell's symbol-coding system e.g. Television coverage of presidential campaign (H.Laswell, Nathan Leites *et al.* 1965). (2) Deutschmann's categories are appropriate if the subject matter is the focus of study (pp. 92-95; 1959).

He has developed eleven categories that cover full range of content in mass media such as war and defense, popular amusements, general human interest stories, economic developments or activities, education and classic arts, politics and government, crime, accident and disaster, public health and welfare, science and invention and public moral problems. If one's content of study does not fall under any of the above categories, one can follow a system that is similar to the present one followed by any of the predecessors. In spite of all these entire one may need, Stempel III suggests to the researcher to create one's own categories based on his problem of research and analysis (Content Analysis in Research Methods in Mass Communication: Guido H Stempel III, p. 123, 1989). "The decision to create your own categories instead of using an existing set should be based primarily on the conclusion that no existing system will enable you to meet the objectives of your study" (Giudo H Stempel III: 1989).

(iii) *Sampling of Content:* In many ways sampling in content analysis is no different from sampling surveys. The most important thing that one should remember here is that the sample represents the population that is intended to represent. The prime consideration, says Stempel III, is that each unit in the population must have the same chance of being represented in the same sample. In sampling of content analysis, there is an additional consideration of sampling time and media.

(iv) *Reliability of Coding:* The fact that the content analysis is defined as systematic and objective means that the researcher must ensure reliability. It means simple consistency of classification. This would proceed usually on developing range of parameters—such as agree, strongly agree, neutral, disagree and strongly disagree or favor, strongly favor, neutral, unfavor, strongly unfavor etc. The primary concern of the researcher, says Stempel III, is to ensure reliability. The first step is thus to work for the definition of categories. The second one is to go over these definitions and deciding procedure generally with the coders before they begin. If one is doing coding all by oneself, the minimum standard would be the selection of three passages to be coded by all coders.

Native and Original Category Constructs Relevant to Indian Context

The originality of the current research lies in choosing appropriate categories and in the construction of categories under various heads. As previous discussed of Methodology and Discourse, the present study assumes significance in the sense it is the first ever attempt (since no previous documented study on this subject is available till date) to follow the broad framework of Berelson, Guido Stempel III and Wimmer and Dominick with indigenous categorization and parameters fitted into it.

Operational Design

Unit of Analysis

1. Editorials, Edit page articles, Press Statements and Contributions by Politicians and Sunday Magazine articles appeared between *December 4, 1992 to January 8, 1993 of Indian Express.*
2. Editorials, Edit pages articles, Press Statements and Contributions by Politicians, Articles in Sunday Magazines, and Interviews with Politicians appeared between *December 5, 1992 to January 13, 1993 in The Hindu.*

Construction of Categories

(a) Theoretical Issues (on Secularism as argued by Political Groups, Ideologues, Journalists and Authors).

(b) Political Issues (on Secularism centered round by various political parties).

(c) Objectivity/Slanting.

Sub-categories

Under the each of these categories, sub-categories have emerged out of the analytical reading of the above sample of content.

Under Theoretical Issues of Secularism

1. Agreeing with Western Secular Model (US and European Model of Secularism of Holyoake and D. E. Smith).
2. Agreeing with (undefined) Secular model of Indian Constitution with strong Pro-minorityinclination (Nehru's Positive Secularism or Dharma Nirapekshata).
3. Agreeing with all religions as equal and removal of pro-minority inclination in Constitution (BJP and RSS School of Secularism based on Sarva Dharma Samabhaava).
4. Agreeing with Secular Model from Atheistic and Agnostic schools (Leftist Schools of Secularism).
5. Agree with anti-Hindu Unity but protect Pro-minority inclinations.

Under Political Issues of Secularism

1. Appeasement of Minorities by the Congress and other political groups.
2. Vote bank politics for garnering Minorities' Votes during elections.
3. Non-implementation of Uniform Civil Code despite stipulation under Directive Principles of State Policy in the Constitution and Supreme Court.
4. Failure to evolve a consensus on disputed structures and shrines in the Spirit of Somnath Temple at Dwarka.
5. Nature of Rashtriya Swayam Sevak Sangh (RSS) and Viswa Hindu Parishad (VHP) their role and character.
6. Communal Riots—*(i)* The role of Congress in fomenting communal riots, *(ii)* Role of BJP, VHP and RSS during Communal Riots or causing Communal Riots.
7. Banning Satanic Verses by the Congress Government headed by Rajiv Gandhi, then Prime Minister of India, to appease Muslims.
8. Reversing the ruling of the Supreme Court in Shah Bano case for Alimony.
9. Opening the gates of disputed Babri Masjid for Muslims to perform their prayers by Congress against the Local Court directives.
10. Opening the gates of the Babri Masjid for the Hindu devotees to worship Rama Lala by the Congress to protect the Hindu Vote Banks.

11. Scrapping the special status conferred on Jammu and Kashmir under Article 370 of Indian Constitution and to make the accession of Kashmir to India permanent.
12. Forging opportunistic alliances with Fundamentalist Muslim Bodies like All India Muslim Leagues and befriending Shahi Imam Abdulla Bukhari, the Head Priest of Jama Masjid, Delhi.
13. Definition of Minorities—Increasing Muslim Populations in certain parts of the country due to illegal immigration—Changing grossly the complexion of original demography.
14. Polygamy pursued under Shariat Law and lack of family planning among Muslim populations.
15. Conversions of low caste Hindus into Islam and Christianity.
16. Ban on cow slaughter.
17. Change of Syllabi in Textbooks of NCERT.
18. Handling of Minority issues and Majority challenges by the Ruling Parties at the Centre (including Coalitions).

Sampling of the Content

The Purposive Sampling is used for the purpose of this study and the sample for the content analysis is drawn from the following:

Primary Sources

1. Press Statements and Contributions by the politicians in the Mainstream Press (1992-95).

Criteria to Determine Objectivity/Slant

Hindus	*Muslims*
Teaching and reminding Hindus and Hindu Cultural Organizations—VHP, RSS, Bajrang Dal, etc. its great heritage of 'secular' credentials.	Not speaking or advising a single word/sentence arousing 'secular' feelings among Muslims or Muslim cultural organizations.
Avoiding answers to the questions raised at theoretical level on the *brand of secularism* pursued by the Congress and other political groups as part of vote bank politics.	Posing as messiahs of Muslims indulging in political gimmickry and appeasement policies pursued by the Congress and political groups, which treat them as vote banks.
Describing Hindus and Hindu cultural organization supporting VHP,	Not applying same arguments to Muslims and Muslim cultural organi-

(Contd.)

Hindus	*Muslims*
RSS and Bajrang Dal as threat to Muslims and national integrity.	zations in so far their relations with majority community was concerned.
Telling the Hindus the greatness of Moghal Kings and how they had religious tolerance as though it was enough to compensate the otherwise damages done to Indian women, temples and property and injured psyche of Indians.	Not being in a position to tell Muslims and Muslim cultural organizations the injuries done to the collective conscience of the Hindus during Moghal rule in India and to advise them to have a broad mind to appreciate the feelings of the majority.
Telling BJP, VHP, RSS and Bajrang Dal that it was mere faith to say that Ram was born where Babri masjid stood and there was no evidence of temple when Babar constructed the masjid there.	Unable to tell Muslims that conceptually Babri masjid is like any masjid whether constructed in the past or now. As such masjid shifting could be possible if they understood with broad mind.
Asking the Hindus and Hindu cultural organizations to give up the issues of freeing Kasi and Mathura temples from masjids unable to explain properly how these masjids came by the side of these ancient temples dating to BC.	Avoiding to educate Muslims that these masjids presence along the side of ancient Hindu temples does not reflect the greatness of Islamic religion and they better agree to voluntarily shift masjids from wherever temples had been encroached upon.
Blaming unilaterally the Hindu cultural organizations alone little realizing that the Courts and the Government's indifference to the issue also complicated matters.	Not advising Muslim organizations to arrive at consensus with the Hindus on all controversial presence of masjids wherever ancient temples existed.
Objecting Hindu Kar Sevaks carrying showels, bricks for Kar Seva at Ayodhya and questioning the bonfides of such actions.	Not speaking a single word against Muslims keeping stones, lethal weapons in the masjids and using them during riots against Hindus, Hindu shops, temples and houses immediately after Friday prayers.
Branding Hindu leaders for giving communally inflammable speeches.	Not applying same yardstick to Muslim politicians who give fiery speeches during Friday prayers at masjids against the Hindus and Hindu temples.
Giving an impression of belittling the Hindus as second grade citizens	Not condemning extraterritorial patriotism of Muslims seeking support from

(Contd.)

Hindus	*Muslims*
in their own country in preference to rights of Muslims and their religion.	other Islamic nations by virtue of religion.
Expressing nervousness and fears that India gets isolated due to Hindus trying to assert themselves and their rights due to them.	Giving Muslims an impression that they need not turn broad minded, have a give and take policy, show tolerance to majority faith, besides see reason in the injured feelings of the Hindus because of the support they enjoy from other Muslim countries.
For Hindus and Hindu cultural organizations, faith should be under law.	For Muslims and their cultural organizations, faith could be above law (supporting reversal of Shah Bano etc).

2. Contributions to Edit Page Articles by the Journalists (1992-95).
3. Contributions to the Edit page by acclaimed authors (1992-95).
4. Contributions to mainstream press by the political leaders. (1992-95).
5. Contributions of academicians to journals and books (1992-95).
6. Editorials of the Editors of *Indian Express* and *The Hindu*.
7. Interviews given to the mainstream press by politicians.

For the purpose of carrying out the study to effectively analyze the sample the following samples have been selected as they appeared in a row.

1. *The Indian Express (December 4th, 1992 to January 8th, 1993: Total 71 articles).*
   (a) Press Statements and Contributions by Politicians – 15 clippings
   (b) Edit Page Articles by the Journalists – 23
   (c) Editorials by the Indian Express – 26
   (d) Articles in Sunday Magazine – 7
   (e) Interviews with Politicians – Nil

2. *The Hindu (December 5th to January 13, 1993; Total 52 articles)*
   (a) Press Statements and Contributions by Politicians – 5 clippings
   (b) Edit Page Articles by the Journalists – 27 articles
   (c) Editorials by the Hindu – 13 articles

(*d*) Articles in Sunday Magazine—2 articles
(*e*) Interviews with Politicians—5 articles.

Secondary Sources

Dictionaries, Religious literature, Books or Chapters in certain Books and articles from Weeklies.

Tests Reliability and Validity: Inter Reliability of Coding

The inter reliability of coding, as suggested by Guido Stempel III (1989), and Wimmer and Dominick (2003) was applied to the problem of research as the number of contentious issues discussed here holds the key to arrive at a reasonable analyses. All the Units of Analysis were placed into Interreliability Coding.

Training the Coders and Coding the Content

For the sake of achieving reliability two graduates with due training on coding have been employed which was tallied with the coding done by the researcher. Approximately 85-95 per cent of inter-reliability has been achieved in the inter-reliability coding using Holsti (Holsti O: Content Analysis for the Social Sciences and Humanities, 167-94: 1969) formula.

Hosti Formula for Reliability

2M/N1 +N2 where M is the number of coding decisions on which two coders agree and N1 and N2 are the total number of coding decisions by the first and second coder respectively.

Validity: Face Validity Through Seminars and Peer Review

In the current research work which is already described as *Descriptive, Analytical and Nominal,* only *face validity* can be applied though the other validities like *predictive validity, concurrent validity* and *construct validity* do exist with limited application in Content Analysis.

The *face validity* has been achieved by subjecting the Inter-reliability Coding for peer reviewing to examine the congruence in the construction of categories. Even seminars delivered on the above research helped test the validity and internal consistency of the categories constructed.

Graphical and Statistical Data for Analysis

The Units of Analysis and the Theoretical and Political issues, besides slanting, would be plotted against each other (Tables 5.1 to Table 6.7) for eliciting the following data of analysis followed by Graphic Analysis (simple histograms and pie-charts). The Data was elicited to the extent of counting the occurrence of the frequencies as determined by Singorielli, McLeod and Healy (1994) in analyzing the commercials on MTV. The researcher feels that given the complexity of the content, which is predominantly qualitative in nature, quantitative data are of not much help compared to qualitative analysis and interpretation.

By resorting to statistical tools like chi-square test, t-test, ANOVA (Analysis of Variance), and Coefficient of Correlation, one need not assume that element of subjectivity could be eliminated. In fact, the entire research of Content analysis goes with the subjectivity at one place or the other.

As such three types of analyses have been elicited from the Tables given (Tables 5.1 to 6.7 accompanied by Graphic Presentations).

- *(i)* Direction of the content (related to identifying the articles based on the content) whether they are Pro-BJP, Anti-BJP Anti-Cong or Pro-Cong or Objective or any other.
- *(ii)* Category related to scoring + (spoken) or @ (not spoken) on the issues selected indicating what issues the authors concerned have chosen to discuss.
- *(iii)* Category showing Agreement with the theoretical and political issues chosen for the study.

For instance + indicates the author chose to discuss these issues directly or indirectly, explicitly or implicitly. It does not indicate whether the author had favorably discussed or unfavorably discussed. It is immaterial. The idea is to see how many of the selected issues have been discussed by the authors and around which lay maximum concentration.

@ Indicated that the authors have chosen to discuss some other issues not listed for scoring. They may relate to issues such as banning the cultural outfits of BJP such as RSS, VHP and Bajrang Dal, dismissal of BJP governments from the states of Rajasthan, Himachal Pradesh and Madhya Pradesh. Since these are the acts of the Central

Government in the aftermath of the demolition of Babri Masjid and not based on any considerable discussion reflecting any differences or agreement on any of the issues that BJP raised all along for over 4 decades, the present study did not include them into the study on the portrayal of secularism in the mainstream press. The scoring of the selected issues as mentioned earlier and categorizing them were considered as enough sample to show how media allowed itself to be polarized and swayed away and how objectively it enacted its role at a time when the nation was passing through a trauma.

Justification of the Sample: The *Indian Express* and *The Hindu*

Two leading English Newspapers—*Indian Express* and *The Hindu* have been selected for the purpose of the study. Further these two Newspapers have been national level daily newspapers with circulation running into hundreds of thousands. Category-wise Indian Express is 'B' grade newspaper with a regional publication—Andhra Prabha—as sister publication and its combined network circulation and sales are quite high than The Hindu newspaper. On the other hand, The Hindu is a national level newspaper with all Indian publishing centers and graded as 'A' category paper though it does not have any sister publication in languages. For the purpose of the study, the news published, the articles written in their Edit page and Sunday Magazine, besides other pages, have been taken as representative sample to make up the Universe of the Sample. In Andhra Pradesh there are no English newspapers, which can measure up to the standard of these newspapers, at the point of time of the study for the following reasons: Firstly, the other two English newspapers available to the readers in Andhra Pradesh at the time of the study were News Time and Deccan Chronicle. Deccan Chronicle which was having highest sales and was having more than hundred thousand circulation at this time, though its circulation was mostly within the Hyderabad and its sub-urbans.

Beyond Hyderabad, it had hardly any circulation. As for News time, it was dominated by its sister publication Eenadu, which was the highest circulated Telugu Daily at this time and, as such, its circulation was limited to that of library shelf across the libraries in AP. It had hardly any comparable circulation either with Deccan Chronicle or with the Indian Express, let alone the Hindu. Further, these two newspapers had no such direct access to such personalities as politicians, journalists, authors, intellectuals, ideologues that are available to the Indian Express and the Hindu which have nationwide reporting network as also publication units stationed in Delhi.

Further both the Indian Express and the Hindu had the reputation of being existent in the Indian Politics for long dating back to the pre-independent times to the post independent era and had the track record of being anti-establishment in exposing the economic and political scandals of the successive governments, irrespective of the political parties these governments represented. Both the newspapers had eminent journalists as Editors, besides their Chief-Editors being the patriots and freedom fighters that led a value based lives. Due to the above reasons, the study was limited to the analysis of portrayal of secularism in these two leading English News dailies—Indian Express and the Hindu. As such, any one who is interested further in doing similar work on the portrayal of secularism in Telugu Press or on the nationwide coverage (entire national basis) could still plan for such a research.

Further as explained earlier, a specific number of articles, covering the crucial period before and after the demolition of Babri Masjid, for each of the two newspapers was selected. The articles were chosen in such a way that they had either covered or reflected the maximum diversity of the thinking on the subject *secularism.* These articles by and large reflected the heat of the times and present collectively the highest ever point they reached in the post independent era.

3

Secularism: Thematic Analysis of Theoretical Issues

Literary Definition

If one takes a glance at the history of the world, especially that of the Europe and the deep West such as US, one understands that the word *secular*, in the sense it is widely popular in the Europe and the West in the past and continues to be so even now as well, has clearly stemmed from an avowed or sworn antagonism against the doctrine of the Church and its growing proselytization of the administration and rule of law. The word *secular* as such is derived from Latin *secularis* which means *the world* not *spiritual* (Philip Bab Cock Gove and Merriam Webster Edit Staff Ed., p. 2053, 1953) .

The New Shorter Oxford English Dictionary on Historical Principles (Lesley Brown, p. 2753, 1993) has given the meaning of the word *secular* as – 1. Of (a member of) the clergy; not bound by a religious rule; not belonging to or living in seclusion with a monastic or other order. Also of pertaining to non-monastic clergy. 2. *(a)* Belonging to the world and its affairs as distinguished from the Church and religion; civil, lay; non-religious, non-sacred. B. Not concerned with religious subjects or devoted to the service of religion; *spec (a)* (of a writer, artist, art form, etc.) not sacred, profane; *(b)* (of a school or education) excluding religious instruction; not promoting religious belief. 3. Caring for this world only; of or belonging to the present or material world as distinguished from the Eternal or spiritual world; worldly. 4. Pertaining or adhering to the doctrine of *secularism*. In the same dictionary, *secularism* is defined as – 1. The belief that religion and religious considerations should be deliberately omitted from temporal affairs; *spec. (Philos)* a system of belief based on the doctrine that morality should be determined solely with regard to the well-being of humankind in the present life, to the exclusion of all considerations drawn from belief in God or in a future existence. 2. The view that education, esp. that which is publicly funded, should not promote religious belief or include religious instruction. The Webster's Third New International Dictionary[13] defined the word *secular* as—*(a)* of a relating to the worldly, or temporal as distinguished from the spiritual or eternal, *(b)* not sacred (Mundane); not overtly or specific religious, *(c)* relating to the State as distinguished from the Church, and *(d)* rationally organized around impersonal and utilitarian values and patterns and receptive to new traits.

From the above-cited literary definitions it is obvious that the terms, *secular* and *secularism* have Latin origin and have been primarily coined to indicate a clearcut separation of the Church or Religion from the State or mundane (worldly affairs) in the Europe (Italy, France, Spain, Portugal, etc.) and then in the West (America especially South and Central America followed by North America). It could also by implication be deduced that the word 'secular' has stemmed from a sociological and revolutionary backdrop in the Europe at first and then in the West, where there was groundswell opposition to the autocratic and despotic rule of the Church on all domains of public importance. What follows is a brief discussion centered on the sociological and revolutionary background of *secular* and *secularism*.

Sociological and Revolutionary Origins

The term *secularization* (a noun derived from the word *secular*) has been primarily discussed in Sociology of Religions, but in history, theology and in other disciplines such as political science and government (John, R. Hinnell, p. 458, 1995). It deals with the social functions of religion and with the problem of personal existence in society. The term 'secularization', used in several different contexts, together with the cognates *secular, secularist, secularism, secularity,* has provoked many-sided analysis mainly directed to scrutiny about the way in which modernization brings it about that 'religious institutions, actions and consciousness lose their social significance'. This impact of modernization may be understood under three heads: social differentiation, also called as *laicization, societalization,* i.e. life in modern societies is less favourable to religion than life in small-scale communities; and rationalization, in which we come to think about things in terms of rational system of ideas, rather than e.g. appeal to magic.

Dobbelaere (1981) distinguishes between laicization of societal institutions, decline in church involvement, and religious change. Shiner (1967) presents *six types of secularization* – decline of religion; conformity with 'this world', disengagement of society from religion; transposition of religious beliefs and institutions; desacralization of the world; and social change. Martin (1978) has called for nuanced interpretation, which respects the subtlety of the subject matter and avoids the danger of generalization. It is against the caution that problems are likely to come up if the Europe and the US offer two differing variations on the same underlying theme of global *secularization.*

It is not surprising that the meaning of *secularization* is elusive when the meanings of Religion are so problematic. The distinction between functional definitions (what a religion does?) and substantive definitions (what a religion is?) leaves many puzzles unresolved. Opposition to mainstream theories of *secularization* has come from Greeley (1973) who claims that the persistence of religion is based on the human need for an ultimate interpretative scheme, and from Stark and Bainbridge (1992) whose thesis concludes, *Secularization is self-limiting. Secularization,* understood as laicization, goes back in its concrete meaning to the negotiations leading to the Treaty of Westphalia in 1648 and was proposed by Longueville (1995) to describe the ambiguous making over of ecclesiastical territories to Brandenburg. *Secularization* also came to refer, in canon law, *to permission given to a religious to live henceforth outside their religious house.*

Used in a broader sense of laicization, secularization is a neutral term referring *to processes in society whereby parts of, or the whole of, society cease to be determined by religion,* e.g. the transfer of secular control of activities – such as law, education and social welfare – formerly undertaken by religious agents.

The neutral meaning of the cognate *secularity* refers to the outcome of secularization, namely human autonomy. But *secularization* can also refer to a process whose outcome is *secularism*– based on a socio-political program or ideology. A classic instance of this use is *G.J. Holyoake's Secularism: The Practical Philosophy of the People (1854),* Holyoake's secularism consists of basically elements of *socialism, rationalism, anticlericalism and agnosticism*. It embodied a *'system of ethical principles'*. Holyoake was a social reformer, especially advocate of cooperation. His memoirs are entitled Sixty Years of an Agitator's Life. His successor Charles Bradlaugh (1995) was a more out and out secularist anti-Christian Propaganda. In France, the term *secularization* was associated with positivism and materialism. Keller (1981) periodized the history of Christianity to bring out the *motif of secularization*. In the New Testament message, according to him, neither the worldly nor the Christian realm preponderates. The second stage, running from patristic to modern times, is marked by the dominance of religious over secular, even the absorption of the latter by the former. Facing objections form the start, this religious view gave way to secularization in the modern era. Scientific truth called into question the unity of the one truth. The church progressively lost its political influence over the State. In spirituality, the detachment from the world is called into question. The bodily and the material spheres were accorded a real value of their own. What is to be the Christian attitude to this process? An obvious answer to this is that the world is to be subordinated to religion or the holy is realized in the profane, i.e. the religious task is the worldly one.

Whereas some theologists, influenced by Karl Bath who set *faith* over against *religion*, welcomed *secularization*, but in a negative sense. More positively, however, the Protestant Gogarten and the Roman Catholic Metz treat *secularization* as distinct from *secularism*, as a necessary and proper consequence of Christian faith. The term *secular Christianity* is sometimes used for a group of theologians in the 1960s based on Bonhoeffer and other resources (Fowler JW: 1981, Boenhoeffer D, 1965). It is very crucial to take note of the kind of world in which the concept of secularization flourished among sociologists of religion and 'radical' theologians in the 1960s and after. The end of the Cold War, the increase in wealth in certain parts of the world especially in the Europe and the US against the backdrop of acceleration of technological development and the decline in formal religious observance among these nations led to an increased anthropocentric optimism in many quarters. However this, contrasted with the recent resurgence of major religions in the political arena across the world, must offer enough to think afresh about the connections between secularization, religion and social systems (Cox, H., 1969; Bruce, S., 1992).

In the Dictionary of the Ethics, Theology and Society (Budd, S., 1977, 1991) Paul Barry Clarke and Andrew Linzey (p. 747:1997) described *secularization* as a process of social change in which religion loses social significance. That process may be many-sided and may occur, according to them, over a shorter or longer time period. One important consequence of this is that the religious agencies lose the social functions, which, in traditional societies, they typically fulfilled. More obviously, Paul Barry and Linzey held, that secularization also occurs when religious bodies lose control of property and resources, when religious personnel diminish in number and undergo loss of social status; when religious ideas and belief are increasingly relinquished by the general population and with the growing neglect of religious practices. However, mere decline in the attendance to the Church over a period of time does not imply complete *secularization*. The concept of *secularization* also applies more particularly, to social developments, in the modern times in particular, that are neither conscious nor planned, but which affect the character and operation of the social system. Therefore, *secularization by implication is a neutral term describing a particular pattern of social development. It should be sharply distinguished, argued Paul Barry and Linzey (1997), from secularism, with which, in loose usage, it is sometimes confused.*

Secularization and Secularism

Secularism, according to them, is an ideology, which advocates the abolition of religion and the transfer of the ancillary social functions of religion to secular agencies. In contrast *secularization* is a non-evaluative term describing empirically established social trends. *Secularism* may, in certain respects, have forwarded the processes of *secularization*, but there are other non-ideological forces at work, which have more directly and significantly influenced its course.

Various aspects of social change may be identified as constituent elements of secularization. Chief among these has been the rationalization of social, economic and political organization, and the supersession of traditional procedures in which religious practices and the beliefs were often rooted (1997). E.g. The increased division of labor. Laicization, which is the transfer of particular responsibilities and functions from a sacerdotal class to laymen, is clearly closely bound up with secularization and has usually been a more overtly conscious form of it. A typical example would the replacement of priests and religious activities in schools by lay teachers, which is in different circumstances, occurred in both England and France. The privatization of religion, a process by which religious agencies have relinquished or reduced significant aspects of their erstwhile social and public performances and confined themselves to servicing private needs, is equally seen as one facet of the more general secularization process, and of its more recent manifestations in Western society (1997).

In recent Western history, secularization has occurred as religion lost its former presidency over other institutions. In the past, secular activities of the people were to be authorized by the Church or religious authorities. The schools and the universities worked under the nose of the Churches as they considered 'Knowledge' as Divine and Religious exclusively. But this scenario changed after the French Revolution and the formation of a democratic government in the USA. Governments came to be elected by the people by popular mandate. As such the legitimization of the governance by the Church became irrelevant once for all. The maintenance of social control is concern of a wide variety of specialist agencies of the judiciary and the police, who have recourse to a battery of electronic and bureaucratic devices, from data retrieval systems and traffic lights to fiscal records and, in some countries, identity cards. Knowledge is increasingly scientific and validated by the empirical and analytical procedures and subsumed into rational structures of tested theory, whilst for the Education and Socialization of children, reliance is placed on professional, secular experts. Health is one more area, which was divested of its religious connotations and is no longer dependent on divine interference or intercessorial supplication (1997).

As a consequence of this religion has become increasingly more a matter of private predilection than of public responsibility. This process of privatization has placed emphasis on the functions of religion as a source of celebration, solace and reassurance. Simultaneously, as religion has been extruded from its earlier role in reinforcing constitutional, political, social and cultural arrangements, so the opportunity has arisen for the churches to criticize and even to challenge the policies and activities of governments. Some church spokesmen see the process of structural differentiation as altogether salutary in allowing the churches, now freed from extraneous entanglements, to present a less compromised spiritual message.

Privatization is the restriction of the influence of religion to the private lives of individuals, but even in this limited sphere religion no longer has rein. The operation of modern society increasingly depends on refined division of labor and a structure of roles, particularly in economic activities. The expansion of role systems has been a major manifestation of rationalization, as human activities have become more and more specialized and coordinated as an essentially impersonal system of relationships (1997).

Religion was readily capable of infusing with spiritual values the relationships that prevailed in the older order, but that capacity diminished once a society had become role-articulated. Rationalization, by which men are reduced to the equivalent of machine-parts, has been a powerful agency of secularization at an individual level. The decline in voluntary allegiance to religious beliefs and support for religious organizations provides some evidence of some secularization even though it not the central part of the phenomenon.

In Britain, and in Europe generally, there has been in recent decades a decline in the numbers professing belief in God and in an after-life. Confessions, confirmations and baptisms have decreased per head of the eligible population in almost all countries, albeit at different rates. In Britain, many Anglican and nonconformist churches have closed, whilst the number of clergy has fallen both absolutely and relative to population. Anglicans and Catholics alike find new entrants difficult to recruit and, once recruited, to retain, so that the average age of clergy in Western Europe is steadily rising.

Sociologists have developed the concept of the internal secularization of religion, alluding to the departure from older doctrinal, liturgical and ethical traditions. Thus, the idea of God as exacting father and judge and of people as inherently sinful has lost currency as the secular culture has shifted from paternalism to fraternalism.

Spiritual and Philosophical Interpretation

What has been discussed in the foregoing clearly gives the introduction to the words *secular* and *secularism* as to how it came into the Indian context and social order purely from Western perspective. To be very precise, there was never an occasion in the ancient India for the Kings or the Ministers to grapple with the issues of *secular* or *secularism* as such for there was no word or term as *religion* as understood in the West in India at any time. Since times immemorial there were different schools of thought in so far realizing the Supreme God, who was described in Upanishads (1998) and the Bhagavad Gita (1966) as Brahman or Parabrahma. Indian philosophy roamed through various schools of thought namely, *Saamkhya, Nyaaya Visehika, Mimaamsa, Jyothisha, Tarka,* etc. It even discussed at length the *Soonyavaada* (theory of agnosticism and atheism) and Adi Shankara (1998) was known for his eminence and erudition in effectively countering the proponents of *Soonyavaada* during his times. A critical reading of Indian Upanishads totalling about 108 gives us a clear understanding of the way the ancient wisdom debated about the existence of the Supreme God. The Upanishads, which were part of Vedas (Ved = Know, Veda = Known, Vedas = Compendia of Knowledge about the Prakriti and Purush), and appear at the end of the Vedas, were basically composed in the form of question and answers between a Rishi (Seer) who was considered a realized Soul and his disciples (Chela = students).

The Bhagavad Gita (1966) is also considered as an Upanishad as it was proclaimed by none other than Lord Krishna himself, who was described by the Rishis as Yogeswara (Rishi of Rishis). Another significant feature of Indian spirituality is that each spiritual act is composed of a ritual or plethora of rituals such as ministrations and worship. The ancient Rishis who interpreted the Upanishads gave some exemptions and exceptions to each of the spiritual acts or rituals, which were described in the *Puranas*, depending upon the place and the conditions prevailing that time. No rigidity or harshness was imposed. Though innumerable number of spiritual activities stemmed out of Upanishads, it was clear that they were all aimed at realizing the ultimate one Reality—namely Parabrahman or Soul. They were no way acts of religious pomposity and gaiety. Most of the rituals being performed even today since times memorial emerged from the Puranas and Sastras, and not from Upanishads. Swami Vivekananda's interpretation of Karma Yoga is a classic example of the vision of ancient Rishis how humans can attain *Moksha* (Godwardly path that frees an individual from the cycle of birth and death) by working above one's self or in the name of God (Swami Vivekananda, 1989). Thus Indian spiritual activities were clearly aimed at realizing the Godwardly path, the Ultimate Reality – Parabrhamam. According to Upanishads to achieve this, one need not relinquish home, family and move to forests. Even amidst terrible public life, says Adi Shankara and Swami Vivekananda, who interpreted Upanishads and Bhagavad – Gita as applicable to the changing times, one can attain *Moksha, the salavation,* by increasingly doing things in the name of God and dedicating the fruits or rewards of such actions also to Him (Swami Vivekananda, 1989).

The Vedas and the Upanishads clearly spelt out that there was one Absolute Truth (Almighty or Brahman) which was visualized by different Scholars (Rishis) differently (*Ekam Sat–Vipra Bahuda Vadanti*) and therefore were several ways to reach the ultimate Brahman and each way reflected a particular school of thought. Lord Krishna in the Gita said to Arjuna that in whatever form one worshipped Him, He was accepting it in the same way (*Ye Yedhaa maam prapdyante Thams Thadhyva bhajamyaham – 20th Sloka Gyana Yoga Chapter 4 Bhagvad Gita).* Lord Krishna also suggested that people should not change their forms of worship or belief quite often. He rather had forbidden it (*Sreyaan Swadharmo Vigunah Paradharmad Anushtitaat Swadharme Nidhanam Sreyah Pradharmo Bhayaavahaat – 34 Sloka Karma Yoga Chapter 3, Bhgavad Gita*). Thus in Indian spiritual life, different schools of philosophy and thought existed always together. When Upanishadic age or Vedic age was on decline at the end of 1000 BC, spiritual leaders like 24 Tirthankars headed by Vardhaman Mahavir founded Jainism which was followed by Buddhism around 6th BC. Until Adi Shankara revived the ancient wisdom of Upanishads and Vedas in 7th century AD, either Jainism or Buddhism mostly dominated India. During and after Adi Sankara, Jainism and Buddhism had begun to decline and Saiva and Vishnu schools of thought began to dominate. Thus in Indian context different forms of worship and schools of thought existed always. They were called as *faiths* ('matam'= opinion). They did not exist under any doctrine as *secularism* as found under the preamble of Indian Constitution after 42nd amendment.

The word *religion*, as understood in the West in the form of a monotheistic Script *with one god and one doctrine*, thus did not exist in India prior to the arrival of Muslims (Moghal invasion in 1525 AD by Babar) during 16th century. Similarly the words *Hindu* and the *Hinduism* too did not exist in ancient Indian spiritual life. Viewed from the Western concept of religion, to be very precise, every *'faith'* in India should be called as a *religion*. In that sense Saivaitism and Vaishanavitism do become religions. Indian Upanishads proclaimed that –*Ekam Sat Vipra Bahuda Vadanti.(There is one Truth – Scholars, Rishis or Gnanis describe IT in various words)*. From this proposition of Upanishads flows the concept that all faiths are equal, none is superior and none inferior. Thus *Sarva Dharma Sama Bhava* rightly epitomizes the essence of Indian spirituality, probably which may be the 'spirit' behind the founders of the Indian Constitution in trying to provide articles 25 to 30 concerning religion and religious freedom and freedom to linquistic minorities. As far as Indian spirituality is concerned, this should be the basic definition comprising all schools of thought and worship. It was the position of the Indian spirituality prior to the invasion by Mughals into India, followed by the Dutch, French, Portuguese and British, and it continued to be so all through the tormenting phase of India for 6 centuries.

When the question of *religion* in the sense of the West did not exist in India, the question of *secular* living and *secularization* of society as conceived in the West too did not arise logically if the import of the term *secular* mainly concerns with the tolerance of other schools of thought or faith in God. The reason for this obvious inference is that even before the other monolithic religions like Islam and Christianity stepped on to the Indian soil, Indians learnt to coexist peacefully with the people adopting different schools of philosophy and God, including atheists and agnostics.

Though incidents of clashes and conflicts between Saiva and Vaishnava cults were reported in the South especially, successive religious heads commencing from Adi Shankara propounded and supported that both Shiva and Vishnu relate to same Supreme Reality. Barring a few scarry incidents limited to South, by 11th century AD entire India got unified on the popular edict that all forms of worship and worship of all Gods pertain to same Supreme Reality. Though the rulers, namely the Kings or persons authorized by the Kings, ruled independently different domains of India, there was equal treatment for Siva and Vishnu under any King's rule. Though religion and State got mixed and the King's life and the religious rituals overrode right from the Coronation to Abdication, there was no occasion for the people of India to invoke the principle of *secularity* or *secularization* as conceived in the West to decrease the effect of religion on the administration and to gradually separate the administration from the State. As far as *secular* and *secularization* are concerned, the following would fairly reflect the position of India and that of Indians as on the date of formation of Union of India with the concomitant and indispensable separation of Pakistan.

Secular Characters of India as on the August 15, 1947

1. Tolerance of other faiths and rituals was already an inherent spirit and way of life of Indians prior to the arrival of new faiths like Islam and Christianity, as many faiths, each of which could be considered as a *religion*, peacefully coexisted here.
2. There was no term or idea as *religion* in India, as conceived by monotheistic faiths in the West, before the Mughal invasion. On the other, there was a term called 'faith'.
3. There was no demand anywhere seeking for separation of State from the Worship or Spiritual activities such as Rituals in India in the past.
4. The Indian kings were never dictated or bound by the Spiritual dogmas or edicts of their spiritual masters like the dominance of Church in the West prior to Martin Luther King's revolt against the Catholic dogmas and doctrines. Eg. Raja Raja Narendhra who ruled Rajahmundry during 11th century did not heed to his spiritual master's advice and married a girl who was to marry his son. This is only an example of the freedom the kings in ancient India enjoyed above the edicts of spiritual masters.
5. There were occasions when the kings embraced different faiths at different times. For instance Raja Raja Chola II embraced Saivism when he was ruler of Tanjore and constructed the biggest Shiva Shrine called Brihadeeswaralayam. After he was driven away by Bahumani Sultans, he moved to Kathiawad in Gujarat where he patronized Jainism and constructed historical Jain temples.

Constitutional

The Indian Constitution provided the right to Freedom of Conscience, Freedom to Practice and Propagate one's Religion under Article 25. It further conferred the freedom to manage the religious affairs. Article 27 of the Indian Constitution provided for Freedom to pay taxes for promotion of any particular religion. Similarly, the Article 28 offered the Freedom as to attendance at religious instruction or religious worship in certain educational institutions. The Indian Constitution has especially provided for protecting the *"Cultural and Educational Interests"* with Article 29 for the Protection of Interests of linguistic and religious minorities and Article 30 for the Rights of religious and linguistic minorities to establish and administer educational institutions.

As was already mentioned in the introduction, the Indian Constitution was quite vague on the meaning of the word *secular* from which flows the term *secularism* (Durga Das Basu, 1993). The Constituent Assembly debate on Draft Article 25 (then 19) clearly indicated that it was not intending to discuss or conceive a Constitution devoid of religion. "We have certainly declared that India should be a *secular* State...But (H.V. Kamat, p. 57, 1995) ....To my mind a *secular* state is neither a Godless state, nor irreligious, nor an anti-religious state (H.V. Kamat, 1995). Echoing similar views, Rajagopalachari stated that, "And if India's government is to be an institution integrated with her people's lives, if it is to be a true democracy and not superimposed Western institutions stated in Indian dress, religion must have an important and recognized place in it, with impartiality and equal reverence for all creeds and denominations prevalent in India (D.E. Smith, 1963)." Asserting the position taken by Rajagopalachari, S.Radhakrishnan expressed that, "it may appear as somewhat strange that our government should be a secular one, while our culture is rooted in spiritual values. Secularism here does not mean irreligion, or atheism, or even stress on material comforts (1956). It proclaims that it lays stress on the universality of spiritual values which may be attained by a variety of ways." By implication the constitutional makers made amply clear that they did not subscribe for a *secular* character akin to the Western, especially the US, French or British. It meant in short that the Indian Constitution was primarily aimed at treating all religions or faiths on similar lines with equal regard termed as *Sarvadharma Samabhava.*

But Asghar Ali Engineer (1989, 1993 and 1995), a renowned ideologue of Muslims' Rights had held an entirely different view on the secular character of the Constitution without inbuilt special provision for minorities. He interpreted Indian life, both individual and collective, was aggressively communitarian and therefore threatening the Minorities. He thus advocated proper protection of minority rights provided in the Constitution (Asghar Ali Engineer, 1995) in keeping with the promises the Congress had given to the Muslims at the time of partition of India. However, Saral Jhingran held exactly opposite view. According to her, religious minorities should not be offered a protective treatment by the State. She was of the opinion that by conceding protection and special status to the minorities, the State is communalizing the Governance and Polity, which would amount to the contradiction to the very definition of *secular* character, spelt out for Indian Constitution. By implication she opposed the views of Professor D. E. Smith who held that test of *secular* character of a State lies in its affordability of protection and special status to minority communities (D.E. Smith, 1965). By countering D.E. Smith, Saral Jhingran clearly pointed out the contradictions in the thesis of D.E. Smith, who in the same treatise also argued that State should not recognize its subjects based on the religion, caste and creed. Indeed D.E. Smith made two contradicting theses in so far evaluating the character of *secular* State (D.E. Smith, 1965).

Two things become clear from the foregoing discussion. Firstly, the term *secular* as conceived and applied to Indian context by the early makers of Indian Constitution is significantly different from as understood and practised in the West. Whereas Indian *secularism* subsumes equal regard for all religions and faiths, the Western *secularism* implies complete transformation of State into mundane and worldly rendering it free from any form of religious connotations. In fact, Saral Jhingran (1995) in her masterly treatise conclusively proved that the US perspective of the term *secular* had undergone gradual but radical change from the times of Thomas Jefferson, as it increasingly realized with the passing of the time that it was not proper to depict *secular* as irreligious and atheistic (Saral Jhingran, 1995). Though the US did not compromise on the separation of the influence of Church on the State as yet, this change in its perception of the term *secular* is a significant development compared to its European counterparts where they still held the view that State should be *secular* implying a total irreligious character and transformation of State to mundane matters influenced solely by science, technology and commerce.

Coming to the Indian context the above held view of *secularism* as *equal regard for all religions* was not acceptable to many a stalwarts of the immediate post independent era. M.N. Roy (1982), A.B. Shah (1981), V.K. Sinha (1968) and D.E. Smith (1963) openly opposed the view of the *secularism* aired by the eminent personalities like C. Rajagopalachari, Dr. S. Radhakrishnan, Prof. B. Kriplani, etc. cited earlier. D.E. Smith, V.K. Sinha and A.B. Shah advocated the definition and line of thinking proposed by Thomas Jefferson for the term *secularism* implying separation of religion from the State completely with the accompanying *secularization*.

Saral Jhingran (1995) also pointed out that the incorporation of clauses offering special status to the minorities and other communities in Indian Constitution clearly ran against the spirit of the definition of *secular* originally conceived by the makers of the Constitution (Durga Das Basu, pp. 190-91, 1993). If all religious faiths were to be considered equal, there was apparently no need to offer a special status for minorities (Saral Jhingran, 1995). If this were accepted as an inevitable reality, argued Saral Jhingran, then two conditions would arise. One is *minoritysm* and another *majoritysm*. She was of the view that an indefinite continuation of *minority* rights in a *secular* state contradicts the basic idea of *secularism*, which rejects the relevance of religious affiliations of individuals or groups in such matters. She was more particular of this view in regard to Minorities' right to run their own educational institutions with or without State funding. She clearly felt that it was discriminatory and violative of the principle and spirit of *Secularism* professed by the makers of Indian Constitution.

It was argued by some scholars, such as Asghar Ali Engineer, that the special rights of *minorities* have evolved out of special historical circumstances and express the nationalist leaders' commitment to create a united India out of a vastly heterogeneous populace. During the crucial period preceding the partition, and after Independence during the Constituent Assembly debates, there was considerable bargaining between various minority groups and national leaders. As a result *minority* leaders agreed to give up their demand for special electorates etc., and the framers of the Constitution in turn conceded to them a few privileges or safeguards though such an agreement ran against the basic conception of *secularism.* One would find similar situation with regard to providing reservations under Article 16(4) of Indian Constitution for Scheduled Castes, Tribes and certain backward classes. In the words of Saral Jhingran, "To identify a group of persons as a socially and educationally backward class on the basis of its caste for positive discrimination is as much *unsecular* as to identify another group as *minority* on the basis of its religious affiliation, and hence deserving special rights. The two therefore must be accepted or rejected together" (Saral Jhingran, 1995). Simply put, both perpetuate communal consciousness and caste consciousness, which in a *secular* State create conditions quite difficult to sustain the *secular* character. She extended the argument even with regard to the Uniform Civil Code suggested in the Indian Constitution under Article 44 of Directive Principles of State Policy. Tracing down the historic arguments and views expressed by Nehru, Ambdekar and Munshi on the civil or personal laws, which do not form part of right to freedom of religion, she quoted Munshi's original statement in the Constituent Assembly that stood validated even today from the real perspective of the *secular* State. "We want to divorce religion from the personal law, from what may be called social relations, or from the rights of parties as regards inheritance and succession. What have these rights to do with the religion, I fail to understand....We are in a stage where we must unify and consolidate the nation by every means without interfering with religious practices. If, however, in the past, religious practices have been so construed as to cover the whole field of life, we have reached a point when we must put our foot down and say that these matters are not religion, they are purely matters for secular regulation... Religion must be restricted to spheres which legitimacy appertain to religion, and the rest of life must be regulated, unified and modified in such a manner that we may evolve, as early as possible, a strong and consolidated nation," spoke Munshi.

It was the first ever advanced look taken at defining what are essentials and what constitute non-essentials in a religion in so far characterizing the *secularity* of a *secular* State clearly lending a hint to the State on what matters State can interfere with individuals on what not. Though Muhammad Ismail Saheb, one of the Muslim Representatives in the Constituent Assembly opposed Munshi's classic interpretation of essentials of religion from non-essentials of religion, he vociferously argued that personal law is entirely based on religious doctrine. Most of the Muslim members of the Constituent Assembly even went a step further arguing that the right of a community to follow their own personal law should be included under fundamental rights. Though this was not conceded by Ambedkar and others, it was assured that no uniform civil code would be enacted without the prior permission of the Muslim community at a later date. As a result, it was included under Article 44 of Directive Principles of State Policy to evolve a consensus on this issue with the passing of time.

Further, the Supreme Court in the *Sirur Mutt* case (1954), S.C. 282 clearly laid down the law differentiating what constitute the core of religion and what would fall outside the sphere of religion. Matters pertaining to specific rituals to be offered to the God as per the prescriptions of the Agama Sastra or the priests of the temple cannot be regulated by the State. But the temple administration such as collection of money on Darshan Tickets, offering Prasadam to the devotees, salaries of the employees of temple, temple cleanliness etc. are the matters which fall outside the religion or the prescriptions of the religion in the worship of God and therefore could be regulated by the State by appropriate law. Supreme Court also further stated that religious reforms falling outside the core of religion could be regulated by the State as well. For instance untouchability or probihition of Harijans into temple is a matter of social reform and therefore State can regulate laws to prohibit such uncivilized practices though earlier they were considered as part of religion. (G.C. Venkata Subba Rao: Indian Constitutional Law, Vol. II—Commentaries, pp. 525-27, 1971). Saral Jhingran not only tried to echo the arguments of Munshi mentioned in the foregoing but also tried to theorize on Secularism by dwelling on what constitute core of Hindu religious matters and Islamic tenets. In the process, she was of the view that both the Hindus and Muslims stop arguing on every thing offending the religious sentiments of the people. According to her such an understanding of separation of core religious matters from temporal activities would help solve problems like reversing the judgment of Shah Bano case by an amendment to Constitution in Parliament, banning Satanic Verses, ban on cow slaughter and controversy over singing Vandemataram in the schools. In the view of T.N. Madan (Secularism in its Place: Religion in India, pp. 547-562, 1992), such an exercise is fraught with a number of questions than answers. Firstly, according to T.N. Madan the main objection to such a separation is from Muslims themselves.

Especially Muhammad Iqbal occupies a very special place as an interpreter of Islam in South Asia. "In Islam the spiritual and the temporal are not two distinct domains, and the nature of an act, however secular in its import, is determined by the attitude of mind with which the agent does it....In Islam it it is the same reality which appears as the Church looked at from one point of view and the State from another.....The Ultimate Reality, according to Quran, is spiritual and its life consists in its temporal activity. The spirit finds its opportunities in the natural, the material and the *secular*. All that is secular is therefore sacred in the roots of its being.... There is no such thing as a profane world. All is holy ground", quoted T.N. Madan. In short, the *secular* is encompassed by the sacred, described T.N. Madan. He also quoted Fazlur Rahman's stiff opposition to secularism which according to Rahman 'destroys the sanctity and university (transcendence) of all moral values.'

In a way T.N. Madan tried to draw parallel between Gandhi and Iqbal. Gandhi also believed that every tiniest act of him was governed by the God and the religion. In fact Gandhi's famous statement, 'those who say that religion has nothing to do with politics do not know what religion is' is cited as best example for comparison by T.N. Madan. In fact life was considered wholly sacred both during Vedic times and afterwards, and Anushtan Vedanta (Practical Vedanta application in life) is what is considered as the real practice of Vedanta in those days. In later years the Vedic times gave way to many more new schools of thought and in the process new ideas and practices replaced some of the old and traditional (Swami Vivevakanada). T.N. Madan therefore opined that *secularism* as conceived and imagined as 'equality of all religions' or in the narrow sense as 'neutrality of religions' has failed in India. He thus suggested that the only way *secularism* may succeed would be to take both religion and secularism seriously and not reject the former as superstition and reduce the latter to a mask for communalism or mere expediency. According to him, *secularism* would have to imply that those who profess no religion have a place in society euqal to that of others, not higher or lower.

Taking a dig at the Left Secularists Dharma Kumar (Left Secularists and Communalism: Economic and Political Weekly, July 9, 1994) said that, 'The Left Secularists' version of Indian history is not only seriously flawed, it also bad politics as its alienates many Hindus who may otherwise support a 'secular' polity. Obliterating the vast differences between Islam and Hinduism by a stress on Syncretism and 'composite culture', as they do, drains Indian history of much of its meaning. 'Tracing out the Left Secularists' model of 'communalism' as an outcome of British Colonialism, Dharma Kumar questioned the many premises of the Left Secularists such as branding the caste Brahmins as oppressors and the lower castes as oppressed in a bid to 'appropriate history' to look quite modern. He even questioned the wisdom of calling Tughlaqs, Lodis and Mughals a 'minority' religion and would not hesitate to admit how dangerous it would be politically to raise such questions. Dharma Kumar quoted Aziz Ahmad's writing in which he endorsed statement of the Englishman in 1892 that 'Islam is in most respects the very antithesis of Hinduism'.

He pointed out that Muslim rulers ruled far longer than the British and they did not subscribe to modern notions of neutrality in State policy however much they recognized political exigencies. This simple fact has surely left a deep impact on the consciousness of both Muslims and the Hindus. Historians will have to overcome this lack of accounts of how Hindus felt, and the paucity of descriptions of life as it was actually lived in the medieval period, asserted Dharma Kumar.

He advocated for a deeper study on the subject and suggested further research indeed on the partial views taken by Left Secularists. He also opined that many academicians could not come forward for a better theorization and synthesis on the issues of *secularism* and the nature of *secular* State for fear of bring branded as a *non-secular* by a group of Leftis Secularists, comprising historians mainly drawn from Jawaharlal Nehru University and Delhi University, whose pet subject is 'communalism project' and are united on the theory of 'historical materialism'. They are the most powerful intellectuals in India.

In fact, there is no unanimity on the definition 'communalism' among the intellectuals. Whereas Left Secularists described 'communalism' as 'revivalism of past culture and traditions attributable to religion (S. Gopal: Anatomy of a Confrontation – The Babri Masjid – Ramajanmabhoomi, 1993; Saral Jhingran, 1995) Sujata Patel argued that "it was necessary to shift the analysis of 'communalism' from an examination of its materialist base to an evaluation of its growth as an ideological-political discourse in order to understand how it was encoded within the discourse of nationalism and how it enhanced its autonomy and affected social processes" (Sujata Patel: On the Discourse of Communalism in The Region, Religion, Caste, Gender and Culture in Contemporary India, Vol. 3, Chapter 3, pp. 145-178, 1996).

Nasir Tyabji (Political Economy of Secularism: Rediscovery of India, Economic and Political Weekly, July 9, 1994) also concurred with the views of Dharma Kumar and Sujata Patel. He not only tried to trace the origins of 'communalism' to the era of Muslim rulers but also established how the Congress having failed in its economic and social policies began to yield itself to sectarian demands especially of the Muslims in order to counter the growing effect of Communists on peasants and farmers. Nasir Tyabji wrote that "As a political response to the erosion of its electoral base, the Congress had, even in the time of Nehru, been resorting to the encouragement of precisely these conceptions of Indian nationhood..... During the Nehruvian period, this compromise with the secular conception of the nation took place primarily in response to the alienation of the peasantry, artisans and lower level employees of the ex-zamindari structure from the Congress, and dates from the time of the second general elections in 1957. Steps were taken to use the residue of a specific Muslim identity consciousness among a section of them in order to create a political challenge to the increasing left-wing influence.... These kinds of political action represented the injection of religion into politics in a manner qualitatively different to Gandhi's."

Even Mushirul Hasan in his article, 'The Changing Position of the Muslims and the Political Future of Secularism in India' (The Region, Religion, Caste, Gender and Culture in Contemporary India. Vol. 3, Chapter 5, pp. 200-28, 1996) clearly concurred with the above views and also stated that, 'Jawaharlal Nehru's endeavour to give a secular thrust to government policies was thwarted by his own party's ambivalence towards the very conception of civil society based on secularism.' While Mushirul Hasan was not inclined to subscribe to the stated position of *Sarvadharma Samabhav* as it according to him was a clandestine sanction or approval of caste system inherent in Indian religious traditions. Nor does he accept the *Dharma Nirapekshata* as it amounted to State Neutrality on Religion, a fact which would not go well with the Muslims as pointed out by T.N. Madan. On the other Arun Patnaik and K.S.R.V.S. Chalam in their jointly authored article, 'The Ideology and Politics of Hindutva' (The Region, Religion, Caste, Gender and Culture in Contemporary India, Chapter 7, Vol. 3, pp. 252-280) vindicated the ambivalent stand of the Congress in wooing both the Muslims and the Hindus alternatively in a bid to give the contour of *secularism* or neutrality of State. They also tried to show how Leftists isolated themselves from popular religion by adopting a reductionist economistic approach in order to counter the fundamentalist forces. In the process they forgot to realize the impact of culture and non-class identities. The Left also failed to disseminate between the elite religion and the religion of the masses. Thus, Leftists failed to disseminate a secular value system through their cadres, they analyzed. As with the Congress, the Left forces were compelled to depend on the State to safeguard the polity when it became engulfed in communal crisis.

Dwelling at length on the ideological bases of Hindutva and BJP's ideology vis-a-vis Congress policies, Sudipta Kaviraj (Religion, Politics and Modernity: Crisis and Change in Contemporary India: Chapter 14, pp. 295-316, 1995) too favoured a solution to the vexed issue of identifying the right definition of *secularism* by shifting the line between the sacred and the profane and playing opportunistically with it which in the long run might erase the distinction itself and turn eventually to more *secular* forms of mobilization. At the same time, the author was cautious suggesting that this experiment may misfire as happened in Iran giving way to religious consciousness to turn modernized ideological form that proves to be more stable than the traditional form and go against all principles of modernity including democracy itself. Rajeev Bhargava (Religious and Secular Identities: Crisis and Change in Contemporary India, Chapter 15, pp. 317-4347, 1995) argued on similar lines suggesting that '...An alternative response does not attempt to seal off religion from modernity, or tradition from *secularism*. Rajiv Bhargava (Giving Secularism its Due: Economic and Political Weekly, July 9, pp. 1784-1791, 1994), in his attempt to bring out an ideal form of *secularism* to

India attempted to classify *Secularism* into various forms such as *ethical secularism* and *political secularism* each trying to project out 'neutrality' in its own way. Procedural neutrality and political neutrality are two more new terms introduced in resolving a working definition for an apt form of *secularism* that befits Indian context most. While proposing these, Rajeev Bhargava dwelt at length the earlier schools of classification such as one proposed by Saral Jhingran—separation of core religious activities from temporal. But in his highly critical and considered analysis, he found such a separation would create more problems than offering solutions and would not curry favour with both the Hindus as well as Muslims. It is the first ever attempt to offer a constructive and deeper treatment to the subject of *secularism* and contained a number of insights though it may be difficult to implement practically. Partha Chatterjee (*Secularism* and Toleration: Economic and Political Weekly, July 9, pp. 1768-1777, 1994) argued that the State should assume the duty to ensure policies of religious toleration failing which a Hindu right would not only deflect the accusations of being anti-secular but even use the arguments for interventionist secularizations to promote intolerance and violence against minorities. The minorities intolerance towards books like Satanic Verses of Salman Rushdie or Da vanci Code matched with the State intoleration in the sense orders banning the books and the film would definitely enrage the Hindu right, argued Partha Chatterjee implicitly. While Achin Vanaik (Situating Threat of Hindu Nationalism: Problems with Fascist Paradigm, Economic and Political Weekly, July 9, 1729-1748, July 9, 1994) clearly deduced by his excellent critique that Hindu nationalism is to be seen as a specific Indian manifestation of a generic phenomenon but not one that belongs to the genus of fascism. It is a pointer in the right direction as Left secularists and Islamic ideologues tried to brand the BJP's assertion of Sarva Dharma Sama Bhava as an aggressive communalism and fundamentalism. Many described BJP's Ayodhya issue coupled with Rath Yatra as a Nazism and Fascism. Working out a theory on this, Achin Vanaik stated that, "Any attempt to theorise the phenomenon of fascism and render it serviceable for contemporary purposes, such as the analysis of Hindu nationalism, must cope with the necessity and difficulty of establishing a 'fascist minimum' which embodies the main dynamics of fascism and is accepted as a dominant model amidst competing theories." Akeel Bilgrami (Two Concepts of *Secularism*: Reason,

Modernity and Archimedean Ideal, Economic and Political weekly, July 9, pp. 1749-1761, 1994) too remained critical of Nehru's paradigm of modernity and scientific temper replacing the traditions and culture. Bilgrami on the other advocated sufficient space for evolving modern institutions and attitudes. Akeel Bilgrami rather proposed an alternative conception of secularism seeking by a posited process of reflection and internal negotiation to arrive at a dialectical outcome uncoutenanced either by Nehru or by the extravagantly extrapolative critiques of Nehru.

Against the backdrop, it becomes obvious how the term *secular* incorporated in Indian Constitution had unleashed a wide carpet for each individual and political group to give its own interpretation and dimension to it leading to chaos and confusion. A lot of terminology emeged from differing individuals, ideologues, political schools of thought both in the run up to the demolition of Babri Masjid and after. Media became a powerful tool in transmitting these across and in the process got itself subsumed by the political polarizations. In order for determining the *objectivity* that could have well been used in the *gatekeeping* by the media to overcome polarizations on the sidelines of the political parties, the following discourse has been used to determine what constituted 'slant' or deviant from 'objective' interpretation of what is the right 'import' of *secularism* or *secular polity* that the people and the nation would have ideally looked forward to instead of what was churned out shrouded in vagueness every form of media and in every minute of confrontation between political groups.

Deterimining Objectivity in Interpretations

Further for the purpose of establishing the *objectivity* and to establish or determine the extent of shift or slant in the used terminology related to *secularism* in the Media from the objective interpretation, standard definitions and interpretations as emanated from the Upanishads (1998) and the Bhagavad Gita (1966) and as explained by Adi Shankara (1998) and Swami Vivekananda (1989) are taken into consideration for the side of the Hinduism (which is not a religion in any sense of the word, but is considered as a commonness among all the faiths that profess and practice with the Hindu Gods as deities). Since the issues on *secularism* are raised by the BJP, which along with its cultural outfits such as RSS, VHP and Bajrang Dal claim to represent the true *secular* life of *Hiduism*, opposing the brand of *secularism* followed by the Congress and the other Leftist political groups as *pseudo secularism,* the arguments of its ideologue K.R. Malkani as presented in his article *Significance of Ayodhya* (Indian Express, December 1992) and the views of Mr. Atal Behari Vajpayee as delivered in his address in the Dr. Rajendra Prasad Memorial Lecture organized by All India Radio, Bhopal was also taken as base to determine the objectivity. In other words *Sarvadharma Samabhava* is pitted against *Panth Nirapekshata* the positive Secularism of Nehruvian times.

On the side of Islam, the interpretations of Islam, as accepted and put forward by ideologues like Asghar Ali Engineer (1989), have been taken into consideration to determine the degree of objectivity and slant or shift from the standard interpretations by different ideologues of different political parties *vis-a-vis* West as also Indian.

The methodology have been considered to establish whether the political groups as reported in the press or the press itself by virtue of its Editorials had indulged in slanting and travesty while portraying the *secular* aspects and what they deem as really *secular per se*. For instance, while blaming BJP or VHP or RSS or Bajrang Dal or Shiv Sena as Communal or accusing them as Nazis, Fascists, fundamentalists, what has been considered as standard base for *secular* credentials by the non-BJP political groups such as Congress, Janata Dal, Lok Dal, Samajwadi Party, etc.? Do they mean that BJP, VHP, RSS or Shiv Sena are not registered under the *secular* provisions of the Indian Constitution and are not entitled to air their views and propagate their ideologies under the provisions of Constitution and laws enacted thereof? Are the arguments put forward by non-BJP political groups in the Editorials or Edit, Non-Edit page articles, Sunday Magazine articles and other contributions based on balanced approach? Did they show over reaction for one singular incident in the Press for the destruction of a controversial Masjid by describing the BJP and its outfits as Fascists, Nazis, Communalists and above all fundamentalists? Are they effective in countering the arguments of the leaders of the BJP and its allies? Keeping in view of these observations, the following points have been identified to establish how the political parties and media indulged in slanting and deviating while portraying the *secularism*.

These points have been chosen from the entire content analysis, as they appeared to be clear issues of contention where lack of objectivity, slantness and one-sidedness of the press as well as journalists, authors, politicians and ideologues clearly manifest in that whereas the Hindu and the Hindu Cultural Organizations were given a number of advices and tolerance, a similar advice for give and take or religious tolerance was not tendered to the Muslims and the Muslim Cultural Organizations as if there was nothing to call for a change on the Muslims and its leaders side. Such a lopsided approach obviously raise suspicion in the minds of the readers as to why a deliberate effort was made to skirt certain most important points of vital and deep issues that led to the Hindus' collective agitation against the presence of Babri Masjid in Ayodhya and other important shrines of value to the Hindus at Kasi and Mathura. An important effort was made to ignore or show lightly, while accusing the Hindus and Hindu cultural organizations for their efforts to re-claim the Ayodhya temple, as also other temples like Kasi and Mathura from the encroachment of masjids. Hence, the methodology have been selected to show how slanty the approach of the journalists, political parties, ideologues and editors over these issues for one reason or the other.

4

Ayodhya Ram Janmabhoomi-Babri Masjid Movement: A Focal Point

The issue of Ayodhya Rama Janmabhoomi-Babri Masjid shot into prominence the whole controversies by far shrouding the character of Indian Secularism. Till 1984 and after, the BJP (the Bharatiya Janata Party, the second name of erstwhile Jana Sangh, which merged into Janata Party on the suggestion of Jayaprakash Narayan, who steered the famous agitation against draconian emergency era of Indira Gandhi during 1975-77) was only speaking about constructing a Ram Temple in Ayodhya at the site where Babri Masjid stood then in its election manifesto and election campaigns. Beyond that BJP could not make any headway that would give an edge over other schools of thought or political parties.

It also spoke in support of freeing the temples of Mathura Krishna Janmasthan and Kasi Viswanath from the adjoining masjids in keeping with the philosophy pursued by the VHP, Bajrang Dal and RSS the frontal organizations of BJP or erstwhile Jan Sangh. The BJP pledged to achieve this as a matter of achieving twin objectives namely, *(i)* to restore the Hindu pride which was subdued under Nehruvian concept of *secularism* which was nothing but putting up with endless intolerance of Muslims against Hinduism, *(ii)* to restore the national pride by resurrecting the famous temples of Ayodhya, Kashi and Mathura to their past glory. By doing so, the BJP and its outfits claimed that the true *secularism* gets established and entire nation gets united caste, creed and religion notwithstanding besides Muslims getting the right signal that they eschew both intolerance and 'touch me not' attitude towards other religions, especially Hindus. But BJP was quite aware that achieving these was not quite easy (RLM Patil, 1992; Swapan Das Gupta, 1993).

Unfortunately, the nation's political scenario started quickly changing with the assassination of Indira Gandhi in 1984, and the ascent of Rajiv Gandhi to the post of Prime Minister. It was during Rajiv's period a clear pro-Muslim posture of Congress emerged enraging the feelings of even moderate Hindus who till then did not align themselves with BJP though the latter was posing as if it was the lone champion of the rights of the majority Hindus. Till then even the BJP representation in the Parliament was not very significant except one time during the Janata experiment when it got about 93 seats from all over India, most of which are from Northern belt with singular digit representation from the entire South put together.

In 1984 elections held immediately after Mrs. Indira Gandhi's assassination, BJP got only 2 seats in Parliament. It was only in the next election held after 5 years Rajiv's regime that BJP started gaining strength to strength. In 1989 elections its strength rose to 86, and in the elections held in 1991 its strength further enhanced to 119 seats. Nearly 5 to 6 important States of Northern India and West, namely Uttar Pradesh, Himachal Pradesh, Madhya Pradesh, Rajasthan and Gujarat slipped into the power of BJP. From the foregoing it would be amply clear that it was Rajiv's regime, which catapulted the BJP to power in such a massive measure.

Five important decisions taken by the Prime Minister Rajiv Gandhi and his Cabinet Committee on Political Affairs (during 1985-90) proved fatal to the Congress and had unwittingly steered the course clear for the BJP score politically over the Congress and other political groups by launching a massive offence on the secular character of the Congress:

(i) Banning of the book the Satanic vs. written by Salman Rushdie in India.

(ii) Reversal of the Supreme Court Judgment in Shah Bano's case pertaining to Muslim women right to obtain an alimony from the separating spouse under Indian Civil laws.

(iii) Opening of the doors of Babri Masjid in early 1986.

(iv) Allowing Shilanyas in 1989 just before launching election campaign in 1990.

(*v*) Holding discussions with Members of Muslim Personal Board and the Babri Masjid Committee, both of which are fundamentalist organizations.

Tracing the historic developments that led to the BJP's offensive against the *secular* character of Congress, Mr. Arun Nehru, who was a Union Minister, as also a member of the Cabinet Committee on Political Affairs in the Rajiv's Government, wrote an article in Indian Express on January 3, 1993 immediately after the demolition of Babri Masjid on December 6, 1992 (Arun Nehru, 1993; S. Gopal: Anatomy of a Confrontation. The Babri Masjid-Ramjanmabhoomi, 1993; A.G.Noorani, 1993; Mushirul Hasan, 1993).

In his article, he blamed the Congress efforts to appease the Hindus, then the Muslims and after that fundamentalists of both hues. He blamed squarely Rajiv in directing Mr. Arif Mohammad Khan to speak in Parliament in defense of the Supreme Court Judgment in the Shah Bano case. Neither Narasimha Rao nor V.P. Singh nor SB Chavan opposed Rajiv on this issue whereas the entire nation was divided on this sensitive issue of far reaching consequences. Muslims who were opposed to the Supreme Court Judgment reacted wildly to it and even held rallies against it which are mostly politically motivated by leaders like Shahbuddin and Imam of Jama Masjid Bukhari.

Arun Nehru (1993) described the development as follows:

> When Rajiv started election campaign of 1989 by performing Shilanyas in Ayodhya, it exposed the whole game. Irrespective of what Rajiv did, the fact is, for whatever happened between 1985 and 1989, all of us should share the blame.

Arun Nehru further added saying that when Janata Dal won in the 1990 elections and VP Singh became Prime Minister, he pursued the line of encouraging the Muslim fundamentalism. " People like the Shahi Imam of Jama Masjid and Shahbuddin, who by no stretch of imagination could be called *secular*, were pampered by VP Singh as Prime Minister "When the Prime Minister after taking the oath visited the Imam in Jama Masjid and held constant negotiations with him, the implications were serious because it affected the balance.

That policy only made the BJP stronger. Now the moderate Hindu is not going to put up with this kind of appeasement", wrote Arun Nehru.

Arun Nehru further argued that V.P. Singh dreamt of combining the Muslims and the backward communities by playing the Mandal Card. The policy of appeasing the Muslim fundamentalism pursued by him is largely responsible for the situation leading to the strengthening of the BJP. "The Left-V.P. Singh-Mulayam Singh combine by adopting a blatant policy of appeasing the minority fundamentalism, contributed to the resurgence of BJP", added Arun Nehru in his political analysis for the situation leading to the demolition of Babri Masjid. The 1991 election results showed that the moderate Hindus, alienated by the Centrist Parties, veered towards the BJP (S.Gopal, 1993; Mushirul Hasan, 1993).

It was also clear that the Mandal combination electorally did not work. The Janata Dal strength in the Lok Sabha came down to half. The Congress share went up in Lok Sabha in 1991 elections partly due to the second phase polling just before which Rajiv was assassinated by a suicide bomber at Sri Perambudur, Tamil Nadu on May 21, 1991. All this led BJP to gain a lot in the elections and to polarize the entire nation as pro-minority and anti-minority which kind of divide ran quite clearly counter to the spirit of *secular* character of the nation. Mr. Arun Nehru described this situation as 'Balkanization' and regretted the fact that a true loser is Indian (Arun Nehru, 1993; S. Gopal, 1993). Unless the vast Hindu majority was convinced that the Government would stop appeasement policy and be fair, the drift would continue, opined Arun Nehru. True to his words, the BJP emerged with great strength in the immediate next elections held due to the fall of V.P. Singh's Government.

For the first time in the history of post independent India, a Lucknow Division Bench of Allahabad High Court came out fully on the whole issue of *secularism* in a daring manner and proclaimed that Lord Rama was one among 22 illustrations given in the original and first draft of the Constitution adopted by the Constituent Assembly on November 26, 1949. The judgment comprising 63 pages, dismissing the objection raised by the Muslim organizations for permitting darshan of Lord Rama at the makeshift temple constructed at the disputed structure by the Government, delivered by Honourable Justice H.N. Tilhari and A.N.Gupta of the Lucknow bench said,

'Lord Rama became a constitutional entity and admittedly a reality of our national culture and fabric and not a myth.' They further added, 'when Hindus and the devotees of Ram claim rights to have 'darshan' and perform pooja of the deity and the framers of the constitution treated as a great national figure of this country and the basic culture, it is something superficial to argue that the petition is not maintainable and should be dismissed on the ground of technicalities.' The judges accordingly stated that ' Shri Ram, Shri Krishna, Shiva and Guru Gobind Singh' have been accepted as national figures and figures of national cultural heritage and adoration. (Krishna Mahajan: HC Uses Rama's sketch to define Secularism: Indian Express, January 12, 1993).

In a sensational article another noted legal exponent who was also the Vice-President of the Vivekananda Kendra, Kanyakumari, P. Parameswaran (1993) writes, "As Toyenbee has pointed out, every conqueror has done it everywhere. The points of honor and places of worship of the vanquished were desecrated and at the very same spot the conquerors have erected their own places of worship. These are not meant as prayer houses, but as standing monuments of their victory and of shame to the vanquished. So was Ayodhya; so was Kasi; and so was Mathura. There are innumerable others of a similar nature. All of the wrongs of history cannot be erased. No one disputes that. But where deep and wounded feelings are involved, and where the sense of the hurt and shame remains unhealed, is it not human to expect a symbolic gesture of goodwill and understanding?"

Echoing a similar voice, Mr. M.V. Kamat, former editor of the Illustrated Weekly of India wrote an article in Free Press Journal (Bombay, December 17, 1992), "Let it be said even if it hurts many *secularists*. In the last five years, several temples have been demolished in Kashmir without our hearing one word of protest from them. There has been no hue and cry made about such wanton destruction..... We are lectured to by Iran and some other Muslim countries on our duties. Has Iran ever been ruled by Hindu monarchs, and had its masjids pulled down to make place for temples to Shiva or Vishnu?.. We should not bear the burden of history. But neither should be constantly pilloried. There has to be someway to heal past wounds, but reviling the BJP or the VHP is not the best way. The anger of the *kar sevaks* has to be understood in this context."

Against the backdrop, it is clear that the Aydohya Ramjanma Bhoomi issue stood as a rallying point in the history of post independent India for several reasons enlisted above. Firstly, it became a rallying point not because of BJP's own strength or influence among people but because of the immature and unwise decisions taken by shortsighted politicians during Congress, Janata Dal and National Front's Governance.

Secondly, it gave ample scope for the people of India to discuss and debate the true meaning and its implications of *secular* character of Indian Constitution and how the successive political leaders of Congress, National Front-Left combine misused and misled the vision of makers of the Constitution. Thirdly, it helped media to mobilize the public opinion on the issues of *secularism* confronting the nation, the commercial gains and enhanced circulation following the media hype of the issue notwithstanding.

The present study therefore tries to focus on the media role in portraying the *secularism* as conceived by different sections of society namely politicians, authors, intellectuals, journalists, ideologues and editors of the very media itself through the opinions expressed by those sections in the form of articles, editorials and interviews, besides news reports and coverage though limited.

5

Portrayal of Secularism: Unit and Item Analysis of Indian Express

As stated earlier and in keeping with objectives of the present study and methodology outlined in Chapters 1 and 2 consecutively, chief of which is to analyze the portrayal of *secularism* in Indian media in the run-up to the demolition of Babri Masjid and immediately after, the following analyses have been elicited from the Tables 5.1 to 6.11 followed by their graphical presentations to show how media reacted and reflected the chosen theoretical and political issues during the most turbulent phase of India. The analyses were chiefly based on the following data:

(i) By determining the direction or treatment of the content of the articles Pro-BJP, or Anti-BJP, Pro-Cong or Anti-Cong, etc.
(ii) By determining the number of contentious issues identified under Political issues category (See Methodology).
(iii) By determining the slant/deviation from the objectivity on the basis of criteria outlined (See Methodology).

Analysis of the Editorials

In all about 26 Editorials have been selected as Units of Analysis for item analysis. They indeed constituted the universe of sample by virtue of the fact that the names of the Editors who had drafted the Editorials on a given day were not known and that they were drafted by various Editors of the combined Editorial College of the Indian Express representing the national character of the Press.

A critical analysis of these editorials, of which one was before the demolition of Babri Masjid on December 6, 1992 and the rest

Table–5.1
Treatment of the Editorials Taken for Analysis Indian Express December, 1992-January, 1993

Sl. No.	*Date of the Editorial*	*Title of the Editorial*	*Remarks*
1.	December 4, 92	Clear the Confusion	Pro-BJP—asking Courts to deliver
2.	December 7, 92	A Nation Betrayed	Condemning the Demolition
3.	December 17, 92	Political Nihilism	Pro-BJP
4.	December 8, 92	Healing the Wound	Pro BJP—buying its arguments
5.	December 9, 92	Knee-jerk response	Pro-BJP
6.	December 9, 92	A Grim Challenge	Advice to States
7.	December 10, 92	Stop Misusing DD-AIR	Anti-Cong and its censorship
8.	December 11, 92	The Honorable members	Anti-Cong
9.	December 12, 92	Without A Strategy	Pro-BJP & not approving ban
10.	December 14, 92	Congress At Cross Roads	Anti-Cong
11.	December 14, 92	Proceed with Caution	Criticizing the Court's Judgment
12.	December 15, 92	BJP's Many Voices	Games of BJP leadership
13.	December 18, 92	Ducking the Challenge	Anti-Cong
14.	December 18, 92	A Wounded Economy	Pro-BJP
15.	December 22, 92	Ominous Portent	Pro-BJP
16.	December 23, 92	The BJP's Calculations	Pro-BJP
17.	December 24, 92	On Whose Terms?	Pro-BJP
18.	December 26, 92	Meaningless CWC Meet	Pro-BJP
19.	December 26, 92	The Pakistani Reaction	Advice to Congress
20.	December 28, 92	A Strategy for BJP	Pro-BJP
21.	December 29, 92	About-turn and After	Anti-Cong
22.	December 31, 92	Pussy-footing on "Darshan"	Anti-Cong for yielding to the threat of Muslims
23.	December 31, 92	No Case for Snap Poll	Pro-BJP
24.	January 1, 93	Motivated Outcry	Criticizing Pakistan
25.	January 7, 93	Coping with BJP	Anti-Cong
26.	January 8, 93	Presidential Queries	Anti-Cong

Out of 26 the following is the break up of number of articles:

(i)	Pro- BJP	:	12
(ii)	Anti-Congress	:	8
(iii)	Objective	:	6
(iv)	Pro-Cong	:	0

were consecutively afterwards for a month, reveals that the Editorials written both before and after clearly showed signs of favoring BJP

Figure 5.1 : Analysis of Treatment of Editorials—Indian Express Dec. 1992 to Jan. 1993

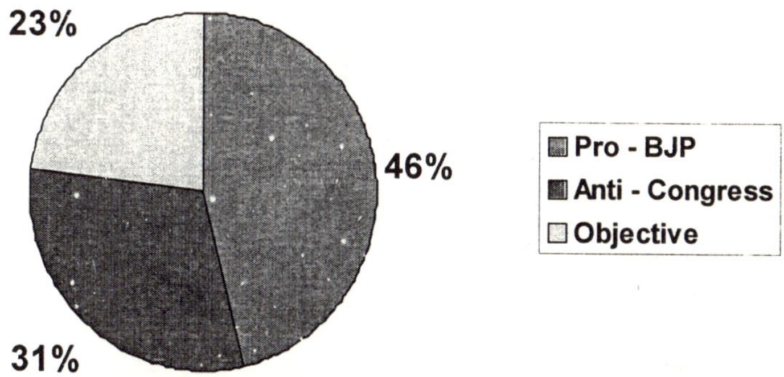

Figure 5.2 : Analysis of Treatment of Editorials—Indian Express Dec. 1992 to Jan. 1993

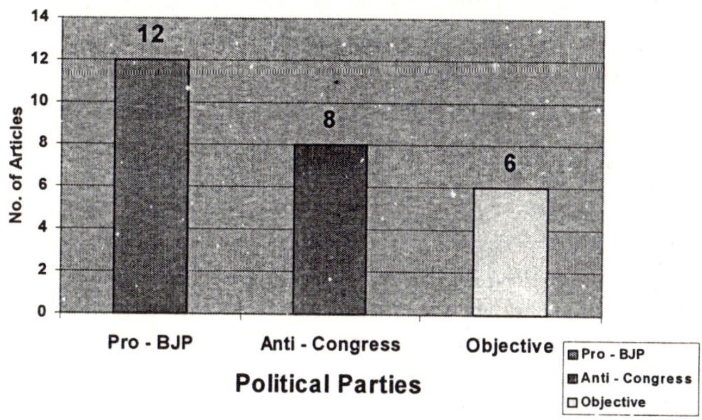

and opposing Congress on the following issues, which indeed constituted the core content of the Editorials. The following list of points favouring BJP and criticizing Congress, for that matter a deep opposition to Congress, would clearly testify to the polarization of Press on the political lines. In fact, the articles which clearly went against Congress in content but no way supportive to the BJP did agree that by acting on those contentious issues raised by the BJP the Congress indeed indulged in appeasement of Minorities giving credence to the allegation that it was *pseudo-secular* in its dispensation. Though these Anti-Cong articles were not Pro-BJP, the way they agreed that these issues established the *pseudo-secularism* would enhance percentage of the total issues favouring BJP (Pro-BJP) to 71 per cent (46%+31% =77%).

On the whole the following break up reveals the extent of polarization in the Editorials of the Indian Express both before and after the demolition of Babri Masjid (See Table 5.1 and Figures 5.1 and 5.2).

Out of 26 the following is the break-up of number of articles:

(i)	Pro-BJP	:	12 (46%)
(ii)	Anti-Congress	:	8 (31%)
(iii)	Objective	:	6 (23%)

In Favour of BJP

1. Not appreciating the arrest of BJP leaders like Advani, Dr. Murali Manohar Joshi and others immediately after the demolition of Babri Masjid (Knee-jerk Response: December 9, 1992; Without a Strategy: December 12, 1992; The BJP's Calculations: December 23, 1992).
2. Not appreciating the banning of VHP, RSS, Bajrang Dal and Islamic Organizations involved in the alleged issue of controversy of Babri Masjid (without A Strategy: December 12, 1992, The BJP's Calculations: December 23, 1992).
3. Not appreciating the dismissals of BJP-ruled Governments in Madhya Pradesh, Rajashthan and Himachal Pradesh (Political Nihilism, Indian Express, December 1992; Ducking the Challenge: December 18, 1992; A Strategy for BJP: December 28, 1992; No Case for Snap Poll: December 31, 1992; Coping with the BJP: January 7, 1993).
4. Clearly stating that the violence in the aftermath of the demolition was very minimal in BJP-ruled states *vis-as-vis* Congress-ruled states (Political Nihilism, Indian Express, December 1992).
5. Failure of Congress and the other groups allied with the Left parties to look at the Babri Masjid issue as a sensitive issue for millions of the Hindus gave BJP a clean edge to emerge as singular champion of the Hindus (The BJP's Calculations: December 23, 1992).
6. Failure of the Courts to deliver the judgment on the land acquired by Mr. Kalyan Singh Government in UP (Clear the

Confusion: December 4, 1992, Proceed with Caution: December 14, 1992).

Opposing Congress

1. Held P.V. Narasimha Rao and Congress, the PM and the President of the Congress, solely responsible for his inept handling of the whole issue in the run-up to the demolition of Babri Masjid (Knee-jerk Response: December 9, 1992; Congress at Cross Roads: December 14, 1992).
2. Demanded the resignation of S.B. Chavan, the then Home Minister, for his alleged failure to protect the Babri Masjid during the *Kar Seva* in Ayodhya on December 6, 1992.
3. Raising questions on the secular credentials of Congress, which wanted to satisfy both the Muslims and then the Hindus to retain their vote banks (Congress at Cross Roads: December 14, 1992; Proceed with Caution: December 14, 1992; On Whose Terms, December 24, 1992; Meaningless CWC Meet: December 26, 1992).
4. Stating that some of the Congress leaders too wanted a Ram Mandir to be built and woo the Hindus and their cultural organizations like VHP, BJP and RSS (On Whose Terms: December 24, 1992; Meaningless CWC Meet: December 26, 1992).
5. Holding P.V. and Congress leaders responsible for not making Presidential reference to Supreme Court on the issue of Babri Masjid prior to demolition under Article 143 or 138 (About-turn and After: December 29, 1992, Coping with BJP: January 7, 1993).

The Editorials however maintained their usual refrain by condemning the demolition of Babri Masjid and glorifying the *secular* polity of India though they did not go into theoretical aspects encircling the term *secular*. It was not even known what kind of *secularism* that the Indian Express conceived as emerging out of the meaning of the world *secular* in Indian Constitution but it wrote "The message must go out that nothing can be allowed to destroy India's *secular* polity, that Sunday's (December 6, 1992—the day the Babri Masjid stood demolished for ever) deplorable event was an act of national betrayal that will not be allowed to be repeated, and that the minorities will be able to live as freely and fearlessly as

Table–5.2
Treatment of Edit Page Articles—Indian Express
December, 1992-January 1993

Sl. No.	*Date*	*Title of Edit Page Article*	*Author's Name Editorial*	*Remarks*
1.	Dec 3, 92	The BJP's Chance	G.M.Telang (GMT)	Anti-BJP
2.	Dec 31, 92	BJP at Cross Roads	G.M.Telang (GMT)	Anti-BJP
3.	Dec 19, 92	Spectre of Hindu Rashtra	Achin Vanaik (AV)	Anti-BJP
4.	Jan 1, 93	The Parivar Project	Achin Vanaik (AV)	Anti-BJP
5.	Nov 26, 92	Ram Temple Inevitable	Virendra Kapoor (VK)	Objective
6.	Dec 10, 92	Aftermath of December 6	Virendra Kapoor (VK)	Objective
7.	Jan 7, 93	Heritage Against Harmony	Virendra Kapoor (VK)	Objective
8.	Dec 11, 92	Unable to Lead	Bharat Bhushan (BB)	Anti-Cong
9.	Dec 25, 92	Choice before Congress	Bharat Bhushan (BB)	Anti-Cong
10.	Dec 12, 92	Exorcising Communalism	Hiranmay Karlekar (HK)	Theoretical
11.	Dec 26, 92	The Shredded Consensus	Hiranmay Karlekar (HK)	
12.	Dec 23, 92	The Ayodhya Tragedy	Ajivit Pathak (AP)	Pro-BJP
13.	Dec 22, 92	Abuse of Article 356	SR Maheswari (SRM)	Pro-BJP
14.	Dec 8, 92	Tampering with History	Asghar Ali Engineeer (AAE)	Anti-BJP
15.	Jan 21, 93	The Hindutva Philosophy	Rajni Kothari (RK)	Anti-Cong
16.	Dec 28, 92	Ayodhya Tragedy and After	Mohan Dharia (MD)	Pro-BJP
17.	Dec 29, 92	A petty-minded leadership	AM Khusro (AMK)	Objective
18.	Jan 1, 93	Congress in a fix	Amrik Singh (AS)	Anti-Cong
19.	Jan 5, 93	Crisis of the Polity	Jagmohan (J)	Pro-BJP
20.	Jan 8, 93	Neither Hindu nor Constitutional Propriety	Amrita Abraham (AA)	Pro-BJP
21.	––––-	Religious Fundamentalism	Ch. Hanumantha Rao (Ch.H)	Anti-Cong
22.	––––-	Significance of Ayodhya	KR Malkani (KRM)	Pro-BJP
23.	––––-	Misuse of History	KR Malkani (KRM)	Pro-BJP

Pro-BJP: 7, Anti-Cong: 5, Anti-BJP: 6, Objective: 4, Theoretical = 2, Pro-Congress = 0 Total = 23.

members of the majority community. Everyone who wishes this country well and holds dear to his or her heart the values of *secularism* and *humanism* that inform its composite culture and are enshrined in its Constitution must pledge to exorcise the evil of communalism from its life stream. And nothing can symbolize this resolve more eloquently than the building at the site of Sunday's outrage, a massive national monument to communal harmony, to an universalistic India

Figure 5.3 : Analysis of Treatment of Edit Page Articles—Indian Express, Dec. 1992 to Jan. 1993

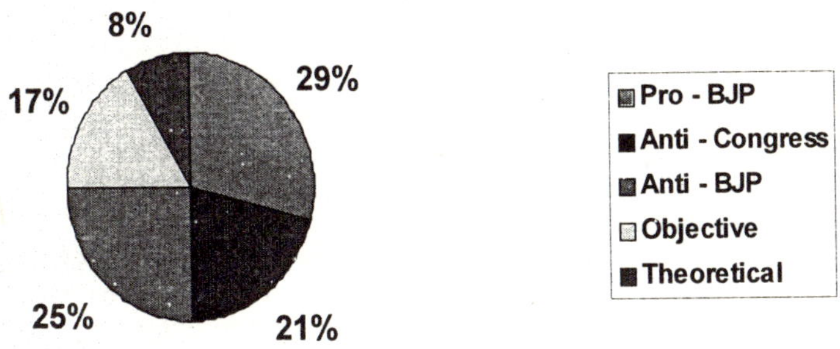

Figure 5.4 : Analysis of Treatment of Edit Page Articles—Indian Express, Dec. 1992 to Jan. 1993

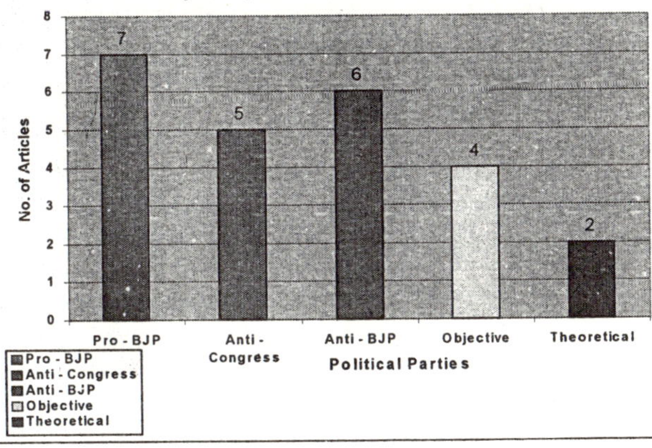

which Tagore visualized, for which Gandhiji died and Nehru laboured" (Healing the Wound: December 8, 1992).

Notwithstanding the above rhetoric that usually all-politicians and media – in a public life speak and write, the subsequent editorials clearly showed the core content polarized in favour of BJP and anti-Congress and its supportive political groups as enlisted above.

Another fact that supports the above contention was the way the Indian Express clearly voiced and acknowledged some of the popular arguments of the BJP and its outfits such as VHP, RSS and

Bajrang Dal by stating that, " ......There is another question that is still more disturbing. The masses arrayed behind the dismissed governments are bound to be restive. Rightly or wrongly, several things have happened over the years to unsettle their minds and leave them exercised over a host of issues of faith and religion ....The sequence of events leading upto the outrage in Ayodhya and beyond has already left a wound in India's social psyche that is till not healed." (Political Nihilism, Indian Express, December, 1992).

Table-5.3
Treatment of Press Statements and Special Contributions taken for Analysis—Non Edit Page—Indian Express Dec. 1992-Jan. 1993

Sl. No.	*Date*	*Title*	*Author*	*Remarks*
1.	Dec 18, 92	Arjun Singh Played Mulayam this time	L.K.Advani	Pro-BJP
2.	Dec 23, 92	Left Logic: Then and Now	K.Govindan Kutty	Anti-Left
3.	Dec 27, 92	The BJP is unequivocally committed to Secularism	L.K. Advani	Pro-BJP
4.	Jan 3, 93	Appeasement Policy has proved bane of the Nation	Arun Nehru	Pro-BJP
5.	-----	Outrageous Onslaught on the Constitution	Soli J Sorabjee	Anti-Cong
6.	Jan 4, 93	Healing the Wounds	Nawab Jafar Jung	Anti-BJP
7.	Jan 5, 93	The Case for Reason: Arguing with Communalism	Irfan Habib	Anti-BJP
8.	Jan 7, 93	High Court Uses Rama's Sketch to Define Secularism	Krishan Mahajan	Pro-BJP
9.	Jan 9, 93	Why Ayodhya is crucial for the Nation	P. Parameswaran	Pro-BJP
10.	Jan 2, 93	How does one repair a damaged Hinduism	Salman Khursheed	Anti-BJP
11.	Dec 19, 92	Secularism: The Fall of a False God	RLM Patil	Pro-BJP
12.	Jan 2, 93	The Solution Lies with the Muslims	MM Sankhdher	Pro-BJP
13.	Jan 4, 93	Shades of Nazism	J.Swaminathan	Anti-BJP
14.	Jan 4, 93	The Frenzied Fringe	K.S.Duggal	Anti-BJP
15.	Jan 4, 93	Metaphorically, we are all Karsevaks now	Swapan Das Gupta	Objective

Pro-BJP = 7; Anti-BJP = 5; Anti-Cong = 1; Anti-Left = 1; Objective = 1.

Figure 5.5 : Analysis of Treatment of Press Statements and Special Contributions taken for Analysis—Non-Edit Page—Indian Express—Dec. 92-Jan. 93

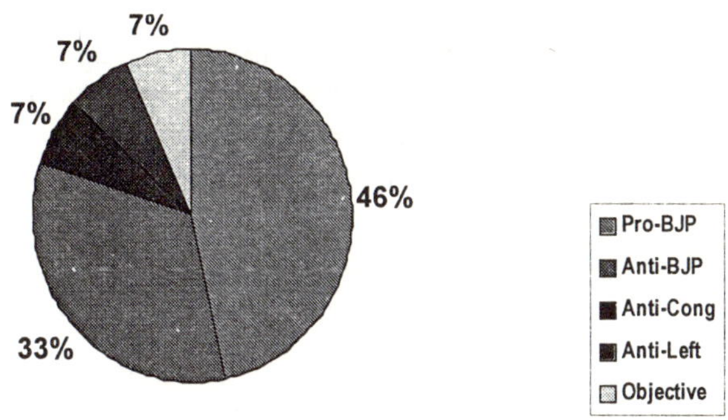

Figure 5.6 : Analysis of Treatment of Press Statements and Special Contributions taken for Analysis—Non-Edit Page—Indian Express—Dec 92-Jan. 93

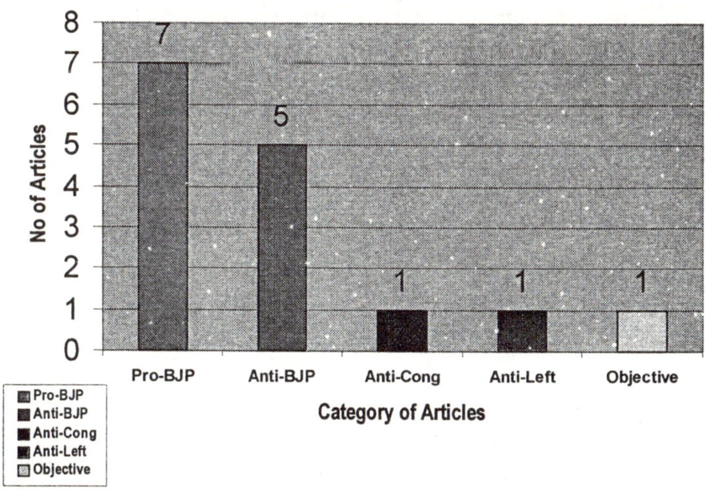

Statistical Analysis

The above interpretations could be substantiated when the Editorials of Indian Express are scored against the contentious political issues (See Table 6.7 and Figure 6.5). Out of 18 selected contentious issues, the Editorials agreed that 8 are truly contentious as alleged by the BJP affecting the *secular* character of the nation since independence.

Analysis of the Edit Page Articles

In all the 23 articles written by 16 authors to the Edit Page of the Indian Express, the following break-up of articles would show clearly the kind of polarization that could be gauzed from the reading of these articles critically and analytically (Table 5.2 and Figures 5.3 and 5.4).

Favouring BJP	:	7 (29%)
Anti-Cong	:	5 (21%)
Anti-BJP	:	6 (25%)
Objective	:	4 (17%)
Theoretical	:	2 (8%)
Total	=	23

Except those which had taken a clear Anti-BJP stand, the other articles which had shown contempt to the Congress also reflected positively on the contentious issues which for long BJP had been harping upon in their favour. Therefore in content the Anti-Congress articles also by and large appeared to be Pro-BJP though it was not explicitly conveyed anywhere thus raising the percentage of agreement on contentious issues establishing Congress and Leftist groups having pursued 'pseudo-secularism .

Table-5.4
Treatment of Articles Taken for Analysis – Sunday Magazine – Indian Express

Sl. No.	*Date*	*Title*	*Author*	*Remarks*
1.	Nov 9, 92	The Psuedo-fascists	Tavleen Singh	Anti-BJP
2.	Dec 27, 92	Regain the Initiative	Tavleen Singh	Anti-BJP
3.	Dec 13, 92	The Saffron Scourge	Tavleen Singh	Anti-BJP
4.	Dec 6, 92	Glimpses of Spicy Journalese	M.M. Sankhdher	Anti-BJP
5.	Jan 3, 93	Shrines in the Shadows	Rajee Suri	Anti-BJP
6.	Dec 20, 92	Outlaws Again	Bhaskar Roy	Anti-BJP
7.	Nov 29, 92	Hindu Pride is no Sin	Goutam Sen	Anti-BJP

Some of the known Congress ideologues or admirers also had at this point of time written Anti-Congress articles squarely blaming the Congress and its leadership for its collective and individual failure to look into the matters, which favoured BJP a lot. Therefore, neither these articles nor their content should be viewed as the outcome of changing affiliation of those in the Congress party. It could at best be considered an inner critique spoken openly through media for introspection. Similarly some of the articles written purely objectively and from theoretical backdrop have to large extent agreed with the contentions of BJP on many issues, though these writers are purely academicians and scholars with least political affiliations. At the same time, in all, a few articles totally got slanted and lacked very much in the balanced view.

For the purpose of the above analysis, the articles of the following authors constituted the universe of the sample (Table 5.2 and Figures 5.3 and 5.4). 1. G. M. Telang (2 articles). 2. Achin Vanaik (2 articles). 3. Virendra Kapoor (3 articles). 4. Bharat Bhushan (2 articles). 5. Hiranmay Karlekar (2 articles). 6. Ajivit Pathak (one article). 7.S.R. Maheswari (article). 8. Asghar Ali Engineer (one article) 9. Rajni Kothari (one article). 10. Mohan Dharia (one article). 11. A.M. Khusro (one article). 12. Amrik Singh (one article). 13. Jagmohan (one article). 14. Amrita Abraham (one article). 15. Ch. Hanumantha Rao (one article). 16. K.R. Malkani (two articles).

The above authors are from various fields such as Journalism, Politics, Universities and Religious bodies and as such their contributions on these issues at the time when nation was passing through a great turmoil must be reflecting the seriousness of the issues and their opinions on the contentious issues raised by the BJP which all along has been accusing the Congress and Left groups indulging in 'pseudo-secular' policies.

As already mentioned in the methodology, author-wise these articles would be examined for its importance on the occasion including the slanted messages and approach.

Table-5.5

Analysis of Political Issues Discussed by Number of Authors—Edit Page Articles, Indian Express—Dec. 1992-Jan. 1993

Sl. No.	*Political Issues*	*GMT*	*AV*	*VK*	*BB*
1.	Appeasement of Minorities by the Congress and other political groups	@	+	+	+

(Contd.)

Sl. No.	*Political Issues*	*GMT*	*AV*	*VK*	*BB*
2.	Vote bank politics for garnering Minorities' Votes during elections – Congress, Left and other Groups	@	+	+	+
3.	Implementation of Uniform Civil Code	@	@	+	@
4.	Building up Consensus on disputed structures and shrines	+	–	+	@
5.	On the Role and Character of RSS and VHP (Communal)	+	+	+	@
6.	On the Communal Riots – Role of Congress (Communal)	+	+	+	@
7.	On the Communal Riots – Role of BJP, RSS and VHP	@	+	+	@
8.	On Banning Satanic Verses of Salman Rushdie-Rajiv Congress	+	@	+	+
9.	On Reversing Shah Bano Judgment of Supreme Court – Rajiv Congess (Vote Bank)	@	+	+	+
10.	On Opening the Gates of Babri Masjid-Appeasing Muslims to do prayers at Mosque – Rajiv Congress (Vote Bank)	@	+	+	+
11.	On Opening the Gates of Ram Lala temple appeasing Hindus and performing Shilanyas-Rajiv Congress (Vote Bank)	@	@	+	+
12.	On BJP's demand for Scrapping Article 370 on Jammu and Kashmir	@	+	+	+
13.	On Political Alliances and Clandestine Supports from Indian Muslim League and Other Communal Bodies – Congress and other political groups	@	@	+	@
14.	On the demand of BJP to check Illegal Migrations and Changing Demographic Dist.	@	@	@	@
15.	On Lack of population control, prevalence of polygamy among Muslims	@	@	@	@
16.	Ban on Cow Slaughter	@	@	@	@
17.	On the Muslims Education in Madarsas	@	@	@	@
18.	On the BJP's demand to check the Conversions to Islam and Christianity – Silence of Congress and other political groups	@	@	@	@

\+ Indicates the issues dealt with by the concerned author directly or implicitly.

@ Not spoken on the issue but chose to speak on other issues like banning the RSS, VHP etc. and dismissal of BJP Governments in Rajasthan, MP and Himachal Pradesh.

Table-5.6
Analysis of Political Issues Discussed by Number of Authors—Edit Page Articles—Indian Express, Dec. 1992-Jan. 1993

Sl. No.	*Political Issues*	*HK*	*AP*	*SRM*	*AAE*
1.	Appeasement of Minorities by the Congress and other political groups	+	+	+	@
2.	Vote bank politics for garnering Minorities' Votes during elections—Congress, Left and other Groups	+	+	+	@
3.	Implementation of Uniform Civil Code	+	@	+	@
4.	Building up Consensus on disputed structures and shrines	@	+	+	@
5.	On the Role and Character of RSS and VHP (Communal)	+	+	+	@
6.	On the Communal Riots-Role of Congress (Communal)	+	+	+	@
7.	On the Communal Riots—Role of BJP, RSS and VHP	+	+	+	@
8.	On Banning Satanic Verses of Salman Rushdie-Rajiv Congress	+	+	+	@
9.	On Reversing Shah Bano Judgment of Supreme Court-Rajiv Congess (Vote Bank)	+	+	+	@
10.	On Opening the Gates of Babri Masjid-Appeasing Muslims to do prayers at Mosque—Rajiv Congress (Vote Bank)	+	+	+	@
11.	On Opening the Gates of Ram Lala temple appeasing Hindus and performing Shilanyas-Rajiv Congress (Vote Bank)	+	+	+	@
12.	On BJP's demand for Scrapping Article 370 on Jammu and Kashmir	+	+	+	@
13.	On Political Alliances and Clandestine Supports from Indian Muslim League and Other Communal Bodies—Congress and other political groups	+	+	+	@
14.	On the demand of BJP to check Illegal Migrations and Changing Demographic Distributions	+	@	@	@
15.	On Lack of population control, prevalence of polygamy among Muslims	@	@	@	@
16.	Ban on Cow Slaughter	@	@	@	@

(Contd.)

Sl. No.	Political Issues	HK	AP	SRM	AAE
17.	On the Muslims Education in Madarsas	@	@	@	@
18.	On the BJP's demand to check the Conversions to Islam and Christianity—Silence of Congress and other political groups	@	@	@	@

\+ Indicates the issues dealt with by the concerned author directly or implicitly.

@ Not spoken on the issue but chose to speak on other issues like banning the RSS. VHP etc., and dismissal of BJP Governments in Rajasthan, MP and Himachal Pradesh.

Table-5.7

Analysis of Political Issues Discussed by Number of Authors—Edit Page Articles—Indian Express, Dec. 1992-Jan. 1993

Sl. No.	Political Issues	MD	AMK	AS	JM
1.	Appeasement of Minorities by the Congress and other political groups	+	+	+	@
2.	Vote bank politics for garnering Minorities' Votes during elections—Congress, Left and other Groups	+	+	+	@
3.	Implementation of Uniform Civil Code	+	+	+	@
4.	Building up Consensus on disputed structures and shrines	+	+	+	@
5.	On the Role and Character of RSS and VHP (Communal)	+	+	@	@
6.	On the Communal Riots—Role of Congress (Communal)	+	@	@	@
7.	On the Communal Riots—Role of BJP, RSS and VHP	+	@	@	@
8.	On Banning Satanic Verses of Salman Rushdie-Rajiv Congress	+	+	+	@
9.	On Reversing Shah Bano Judgment of Supreme Court—Rajiv Congess (Vote Bank)	+	+	+	@
10.	On Opening the Gates of Babri Masjid-Appeasing Muslims to do prayers at Mosque—Rajiv Congress (Vote Bank)	+	+	+	@
11.	On Opening the Gates of Ram Lala temple appeasing Hindus and performing Shilanyas-Rajiv Congress (Vote Bank)	+	+	+	@

(Contd.)

Sl. No.	Political Issues	MD	AMK	AS	JM
12.	On BJP 's demand for Scrapping Article 370 on Jammu and Kashmir	+	+	@	@
13.	On Political Alliances and Clandestine Supports from Indian Muslim League and Other Communal Bodies—Congress and other political groups	+	+	+	@
14.	On the demand of BJP to check Illegal Migrations and Changing Demographic Distributions	@	@	@	@
15.	On Lack of population control, prevalence of polygamy among Muslims	+	@	@	@
16.	Ban on Cow Slaughter	@	@	@	@
17.	On the Muslims Education in Madarsas	@	@	@	@
18.	On the BJP's demand to check the Conversions to Islam and Christianity—Silence of Congress and other political groups	@	@	@	@

\+ Indicates the issues dealt with by the concerned author directly or implicitly.

@ Not spoken on the issue but chose to speak on other issues like banning the RSS. VHP etc. and dismissal of BJP Governments in Rajasthan, MP and Himachal Pradesh.

Table-5.8

Analysis of Political Issues Discussed by Number of Authors—Edit Page Articles—Indian Express, Dec. 1992-Jan. 1993

Sl. No.	Political Issues	AA	CH.H	KRM
1.	Appeasement of Minorities by the Congress and other political groups	@	@	+
2.	Vote bank politics for garnering Minorities' Votes during elections—Congress, Left and other Groups	@	@	+
3.	Implementation of Uniform Civil Code	@	@	+
4.	Building up Consensus on disputed structures and shrines	@	@	+
5.	On the Role and Character of RSS and VHP (Communal)	@	@	–
6.	On the Communal Riots—Role of Congress (Communal)	@	@	+
7.	On the Communal Riots—Role of BJP, RSS and VHP	@	@	–

(Contd.)

Sl. No.	Political Issues	AA	CH.H	KRM
8.	On Banning Satanic Verses of Salman Rushdie-Rajiv Congress	@	@	+
9.	On Reversing Shah Bano Judgment of Supreme Court – Rajiv Congess (Vote Bank)	@	@	+
10.	On Opening the Gates of Babri Masjid-Appeasing Muslims to do prayers at Mosque – Rajiv Congress (Vote Bank)	@	@	+
11.	On Opening the Gates of Ram Lala temple appeasing Hindus and performing Shilanyas-Rajiv Congress (Vote Bank)	@	@	+
12.	On BJP 's demand for Scrapping Article 370 on Jammu and Kashmir	@	@	+
13.	On Political Alliances and Clandestine Supports from Indian Muslim League and Other Communal Bodies – Congress and other political groups	@	@	+
14.	On the demand of BJP to check Illegal Migrations and Changing Demographic Distributions	@	@	+
15.	On Lack of population control, prevalence of polygamy among Muslims	@	@	+
16.	Ban on Cow Slaughter	@	@	+
17.	On the Muslims Education in Madarsas	@	@	@
18.	On the BJP's demand to check the Conversions to Islam and Christianity – Silence of Congress and other political groups	@	@	+

\+ Indicates the issues dealt with by the concerned author directly or implicitly.

@ Not spoken on the issue but chose to speak on other issues like banning the RSS, VHP etc., and dismissal of BJP Governments in Rajasthan, MP and Himachal Pradesh.

Figure 5.7 : Analysis of Scoring the Number of Authors Subscribing to Maximum Number of Political Issues—Edit Page—Indian Express, Dec. 1992 to Jan. 1993

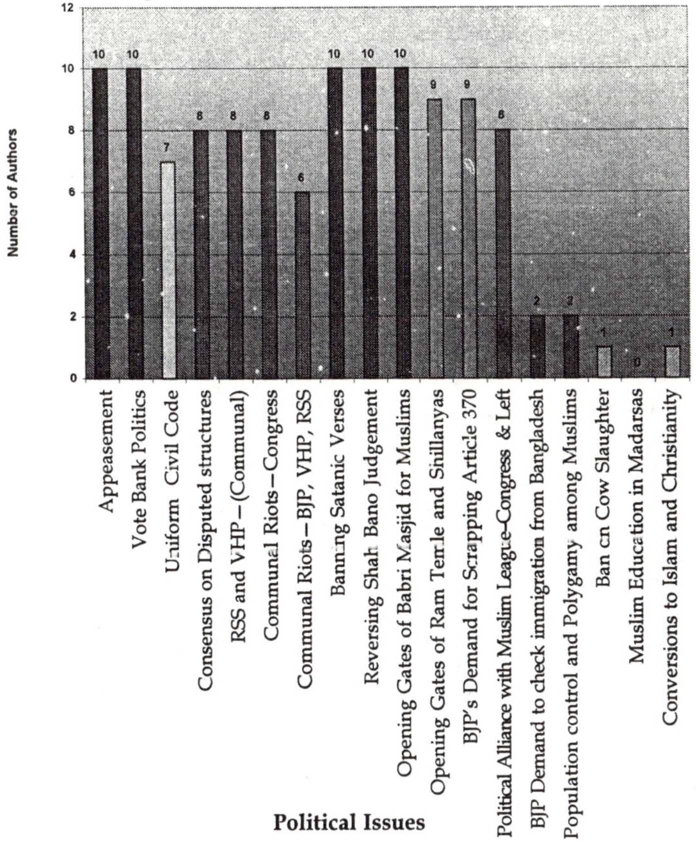

Table-5.9

Analysis of Political Issues Discussed by Number of Authors – Non-Edit Page Articles, Indian Express, Dec. 1992 -Jan. 1993

Sl. No.	*Political Issues*	*LKA*	*KGK*	*AN*	*SS*
1.	Appeasement of Minorities by the Congress and other political groups	+	+	+	@
2.	Vote bank politics for garnering Minorities' Votes during elections – Congress, Left and other Groups	+	+	+	@

(Contd.)

Sl. No.	Political Issues	LKA	KGK	AN	SS
3.	Implementation of Uniform Civil Code		@	@	@
4.	Building up Consensus on disputed structures and shrines	+	@	+	@
5.	On the Role and Character of RSS and VHP (Communal)	+	@	@	@
6.	On the Communal Riots – Role of Congress (Communal)	@	@	@	@
7.	On the Communal Riots – Role of BJP, RSS and VHP	@	@	@	@
8.	On Banning Satanic Verses of Salman Rushdie-Rajiv Congress	@	@	+	@
9.	On Reversing Shah Bano Judgment of Supreme Court-Rajiv Congess (Vote Bank)	@	@	+	@
10.	On Opening the Gates of Babri Masjid-Appeasing Muslims to do prayers at Mosque – Rajiv Congress (Vote Bank)	+	@	+	@
11.	On Opening the Gates of Ram Lala temple appeasing Hindus and performing Shilanyas-Rajiv Congress (Vote Bank)	+	@	+	@
12.	On BJP 's demand for Scrapping Article 370 on Jammu and Kashmir	@	@	@	@
13.	On Political Alliances and Clandestine Supports from Indian Muslim League and Other Communal Bodies-Congress and other political groups	@	@	+	@
14.	On the demand of BJP to check Illegal Migrations and Changing Demographic Distributions	@	@	+	@
15.	On Lack of population control, prevalence of polygamy among Muslims	@	@	+	@
16.	Ban on Cow Slaughter	@	@	@	@
17.	On the Muslims Education in Madarsas	@	@	@	@
18.	On the BJP's demand to check the Conversions to Islam and Christianity – Silence of Congress and other political groups	@	@	+	@

\+ Indicates the issues dealt with by the concerned author directly or implicitly.

@ Not spoken on the issue but chose to speak on other issues like banning the RSS, VHP etc. and dismissal of BJP Governments in Rajasthan, MP and Himachal Pradesh.

Table-5.10

Analysis of Political Issues Discussed by Number of Authors—Non-Edit Page Articles, Indian Express, Dec. 1992-Jan. 1993

Sl. No.	*Political Issues*	*NZJ*	*IH*	*KM*	*PP*
1.	Appeasement of Minorities by the Congress and other political groups	@	+	@	+
2.	Vote bank politics for garnering Minorities' Votes during elections—Congress, Left and other Groups	@	+	@	+
3.	Implementation of Uniform Civil Code	@	+	@	@
4.	Building up Consensus on disputed structures and shrines	@	+	@	+
5.	On the Role and Character of RSS and VHP (Communal)	@	@	@	+
6.	On the Communal Riots—Role of Congress (Communal)	@	@	@	@
7.	On the Communal Riots—Role of BJP, RSS and VHP	@	@	@	@
8.	On Banning Satanic Verses of Salman Rushdie-Rajiv Congress	@	+	@	+
9.	On Reversing Shah Bano Judgment of Supreme Court-Rajiv Congess (Vote Bank)	@	+	@	+
10.	On Opening the Gates of Babri Masjid-Appeasing Muslims to do prayers at Mosque—Rajiv Congress (Vote Bank)	@	+	@	+
11.	On Opening the Gates of Ram Lala temple appeasing Hindus and performing Shilanyas-Rajiv Congress (Vote Bank)	@	+	@	+
12.	On BJP's demand for Scrapping Article 370 on Jammu and Kashmir	@	+	@	+
13.	On Political Alliances and Clandestine Supports from Indian Muslim League and Other Communal Bodies—Congress and other political groups	@	+	@	+
14.	On the demand of BJP to check Illegal Migrations and Changing Demographic Distributions	@	+	@	@
15.	On Lack of population control, prevalence of polygamy among Muslims	@	+	@	@
16.	Ban on Cow Slaughter	@	+	@	@

(Contd.)

Sl. No.	Political Issues	NZJ	IH	KM	PP
17.	On the Muslims Education in Madarsas	@	+	@	@
18.	On the BJP's demand to check the Conversions to Islam and Christianity – Silence of Congress and other political groups	@	+	@	@

\+ Indicates the issues dealt with by the concerned author directly or implicitly.

@ Not spoken on the issue but chose to speak on other issues like banning the RSS, VHP etc. and dismissal of BJP Governments in Rajasthan, MP and Himachal Pradesh.

Table–5.11

Analysis of Political Issues Discussed by Number of Authors–Non-Edit Page Articles, Indian Express, Dec. 1992–Jan. 1993

Sl. No.	Political Issues	SK	RLMP	MMS	JS
1.	Appeasement of Minorities by the Congress and other political groups	+	+	+	@
2.	Vote bank politics for garnering Minorities' Votes during elections – Congress, Left and other Groups	+	+	+	@
3.	Implementation of Uniform Civil Code	@	@	@	@
4.	Building up Consensus on disputed structures and shrines	+	@	+	@
5.	On the Role and Character of RSS and VHP (Communal)	+	@	@	@
6.	On the Communal Riots – Role of Congress (Communal)	@	@	@	@
7.	On the Communal Riots – Role of BJP, RSS and VHP	@	@	@	@
8.	On Banning Satanic Verses of Salman Rushdie-Rajiv Congress	@	@	+	@
9.	On Reversing Shah Bano Judgment of Supreme Court – Rajiv Congess (Vote Bank)	@	+	+	@
10.	On Opening the Gates of Babri Masjid-Appeasing Muslims to do prayers at Mosque – Rajiv Congress (Vote Bank)	@	+	+	@
11.	On Opening the Gates of Ram Lala temple appeasing Hindus and performing Shilanyas-Rajiv Congress (Vote Bank)	@	+	+	@

(Contd.)

Sl. No.	Political Issues	SK	RLMP	MMS	JS
12.	On BJP's demand for Scrapping Article 370 on Jammu and Kashmir	@	@	@	@
13.	On Political Alliances and Clandestine Supports from Indian Muslim League and Other Communal Bodies – Congress and other political groups	@	@	@	@
14.	On the demand of BJP to check Illegal Migrations and Changing Demographic Distributions	@	@	@	@
15.	On Lack of population control, prevalence of polygamy among Muslims	@	@	@	@
16.	Ban on Cow Slaughter	@	@	@	@
17.	On the Muslims Education in Madarsas	@	@	@	@
18.	On the BJP's demand to check the Conversions to Islam and Christianity – Silence of Congress and other political groups	@	@	@	@

\+ Indicates the issues dealt with by the concerned author directly or implicitly.

@ Not spoken on the issue but chose to speak on other issues like banning the RSS, VHP etc. and dismissal of BJP Governments in Rajasthan, MP and Himachal Pradesh.

Table-5.12

Analysis of Political Issues Discussed by Number of Authors – Non-Edit Page Articles, Indian Express, Dec. 1992-Jan. 1993

Sl. No.	Political Issues	KSD	SD	TS	BR
1.	Appeasement of Minorities by the Congress and other political groups	@	+	+	+
2.	Vote bank politics for garnering Minorities' Votes during elections – Congress, Left and other Groups	@	+	+	+
3.	Implementation of Uniform Civil Code	@	@	+	@
4.	Building up Consensus on disputed structures and shrines	@	@	+	@
5.	On the Role and Character of RSS and VHP (Communal)	+	@	+	+
6.	On the Communal Riots – Role of Congress (Communal)	@	@	+	@

(Contd.)

Sl. No.	Political Issues	KSD	SD	TS	BR
7.	On the Communal Riots – Role of BJP, RSS and VHP	+	@	+	+
8.	On Banning Satanic Verses of Salman Rushdie-Rajiv Congress	@	+	+	@
9.	On Reversing Shah Bano Judgment of Supreme Court – Rajiv Congess (Vote Bank)	@	+	+	@
10.	On Opening the Gates of Babri Masjid-Appeasing Muslims to do prayers at Mosque – Rajiv Congress (Vote Bank)	@	+	+	@
11.	On Opening the Gates of Ram Lala temple appeasing Hindus and performing Shilanyas-Rajiv Congress (Vote Bank)	@	+	+	@
12.	On BJP's demand for Scrapping Article 370 on Jammu and Kashmir	@	@	+	@
13.	On Political Alliances and Clandestine Supports from Indian Muslim League and Other Communal Bodies – Congress and other political groups	@	@	+	@
14.	On the demand of BJP to check Illegal Migrations and Changing Demographic Distributions	@	@	+	@
15.	On Lack of population control, prevalence of polygamy among Muslims	@	@	+	@
16.	Ban on Cow Slaughter	@	@	+	@
17.	On the Muslims Education in Madarsas	@	@	+	@
18.	On the BJP's demand to check the Conversions to Islam and Christianity – Silence of Congress and other political groups	@	@	+	@

+ Indicates the issues dealt with by the concerned author directly or implicitly.

@ Not spoken on the issue but chose to speak on other issues like banning the RSS, VHP etc. and dismissal of BJP Governments in Rajasthan, MP and Himachal Pradesh.

1. G.M. Telang: Anti-BJP Slanted

Basically Anti-BJP articles both in the beginning and in the end but agrees on some issues raised by the BJP.

Is faith above the rule of law? This question has been a crucial aspect of the Ayodhya dispute. The constant refrain of the Viswa Hindu Parishad

Figure 5.8 : Analysis of Scoring the Maximum Number of Authors Subscribing to the Maximum Number of Political Issues—Non-Edit Page Articles, Indian Express Dec. 92-Jan. 93

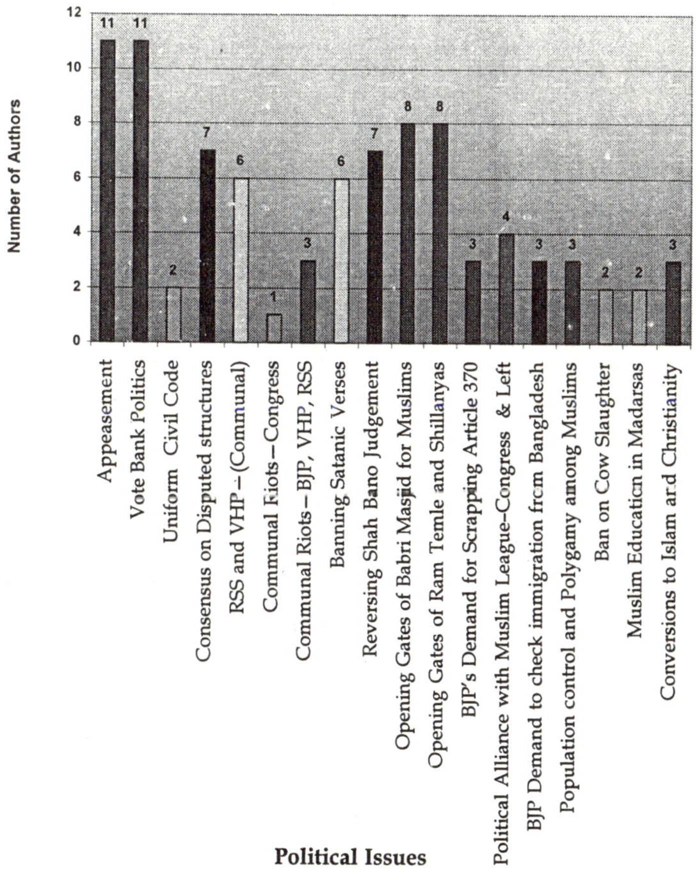

and the Rashtriya Swayam Sevak Sangh has been that an issue inextricably bound up with faith or religious sentiment cannot be disposed by the courts of law.

Slanted

The author begins his article by questioning the propriety of VHP, RSS and BJP's statement that the Ram Temple issue was a matter of faith and could not be decided by the Courts.

The statement is apparently a *slanted* statement as per the criteria of deciding the slanted statements mentioned in Methodology. The author conveniently forgot to apply same principle to the Muslims and was unilateral in his accusation ignoring the similar claims of Muslim organizations (e.g. Vandemataram, Shah Bhano Judgment, etc. This was therefore a unilateral statement to begin with lacking in balance in approach.

Favouring the Issues Raised by the BJP

1. The author admits that, *Many Hindus genuinely believe that Babri Masjid was built upon the ruins of a desecrated Ram temple...... This is a case for patient evolution of a consensus on how best to satisfy the sentiments of the Hindus without offending those of the Muslims.*
2. The author further appreciates the lecture given by Atal Behari Vajpayee on the occasion of Dr. Rajendra Prasad Memorial Series, at All India Radio, Bhopal, December 1992 in which Vajpayee advocated 'panth nirpekshata' as the right substitute to 'dharm nirpekshata' to maintain communal neutrality and pleaded to observe 'sarvadharma samabhav'. He also strongly condemned the attitude of Muslims not to sing Vandemataram and oppose judgments such as delivered in Shah Bhano case (A.B. Vajpayee: Calls for Equality of Religions. The Hindu, December 1992). If the author appreciates Vajpayee's lecture it was not clear in the article whether he was agreeing with all the statements of Vajpayee.
3. The author admits in his second article that all political parties played a vicious role by aligning themselves with religion at one time or the other: *Almost all the other political parties, including the Congress and the two Communist parties, have from time to time used religious, linguistic, case and regional sentiments for electoral purposes, while professing to be mainly concerned with wide political and economic objectives.*

Criticize BJP

1. For indulging in unlawful acts such as violating the assurance given to the Supreme Court and yielding to the VHP and RSS more than permissible.
2. Warns BJP and its leadership about the danger of things slipping out of their control and discipline.

2. *Achin Vanaik: Anti-BJP Slanted*

Two articles were written and both were basically Anti-BJP admits one or two issues raised by the BJP as right.

The article is highly emotive in its tone and written in a one-sided manner absolutely. The following slanted statements are classic examples to show how the article ran lacking balance in argument and emotion.

Slanted Statements

1. *The way the press glorified L.K. Advani and A.B.Vajpayee till recently was shameful. As if political content was to be gauged by the politics of image or media charm. All the leaders of the Sangh Parivar have always been committed, above everything else, to Hindu Rashtra. For all their sophistries about the distinction between a Hindu Nation and a Hindu State, there is no way their version of the former can come about or be separated from the institutionalization of the latter, that is, changing the character of the Constitution.*
2. *The Hindu state, if it emerges, may or may be the embodiment of Indian fascism, it may or may not be some variety of fascism; it may be 'hard' or 'soft'. But even a 'soft' Hindu state means something qualitatively different and more horrendous than the kind of non-denominational state with its flawed secularity that we have today.*
3. *Suddenly more people have woken up to realize that whatever the weaknesses, limitations and even deceits of our version of a secular state it is far more decent and worth of defence than what its Hindu nationalist opponents aim to replace it with.*
4. *The barrage on 'pseudo secularism' is in fact led by pseudo-nationalists and pseudo-sanyasins espousing a pseudo-Hinduism.*
5. *Let us be clear. Behind its peek-a-boo deception: "We will respect the Constitution", "No faith is above the law", "We will only relocate the structure. But it is already a mandir, so we will build around and over it" – the Sangh Parivar has achieved its aim.*
6. *There was never any question of not ultimately destroying the masjid because the central aim was to humiliate Muslims and denigrate Indian secularism, not so much to build a grand temple to Ram.*

7. *It is impossible to whip up to anywhere near the same degree, popular passions simply to build a temple rather than to symbolically destroy the enemy.*
8. *They will continue to endorse and encourage the politics of hate and 'historical revenge' no matter what costs this may inflict on the country.*
9. *In the name of attacking the intolerance of other religions they have promoted their own intolerance.*
10. *In the name of attacking the 'unHindu' ethos of aggression they have sought to instill the worst instincts of aggression among Hindus.*
11. *In the name of opposing the politics of religious-based vote banks, they have sought to establish their own religious based vote bank.*
12. *In the name of opposing destruction of temples they have organized their own politics around the same principle of religious-emotional desecration and shrine destruction (not just Ayodhya but Varanasi and Madhura, who knows where else).*

Likewise runs the endless tirade against the BJP. In all these unilateral and highly slanted statements, the author appears ironically to have agreed with the BJP's statements that the Islam is highly intolerant religion, and the Congress and other political parties have indulged in brazen appeasement of minorities and vote bank politics. Yet, it was not clear why he was against BJP for repeating the same. It appears he wants BJP alone to remain pious whereas all others in certain degree, if not leading to the extent of demolishing somebody's faith, can indulge in such politics. The author failed to establish objectivity, clarity and purpose in his array of slanted statements and accusations against BJP thus.

In his second article too the author marches ahead in unilaterally accusing the BJP and its allies without having a holistic look at whole range of issues and determining who is who and to what extent the correction if required in the polity and Constitution if the things were to improve and to avoid repetition of what happened now.

1. *That is, to try and weld a 'common enemy' for which the most plausible candidate was Muslim and Islam. From the inception of the RSS to this day, hostility to Muslims and Islam has been central to the logic and thrust of its Hindu nationalism.*
2. *But then another problem. How to effectively establish a popular sense of grievance against Muslims especially when throughout*

the 20th century and certainly from 1947, any claim that Muslims were directly oppressing Hindus would appear outlandish even to the most rabid Hindu nationalist?" (Does the author mean that the BJP and its allies are not rabid Hindu nationalists at this time? In that case what is the grievance?)

3. *Two techniques have been developed. One is to cultivate a sense of grievance through the politics of 'historical revenge'. Here it is necessary to establish the 'foreignness' of Islam (and implicitly the 'un Indianness of Muslims) and to arouse as much hostility as possible to the actual and presumed inequities of rule by Muslim kingdoms. In doing the last it helps greatly if domination by Muslim rulers over Hindus and Muslims can be passed off as frequently and silently as possible, as 'domination of Muslims over Hindus.*
4. *But the historical revenge is not enough. Today's Muslims have somehow to be put in the dock because today's Hindus have to be welded together. Since there is no direct Muslim oppression of Hindus, the angle of attack is slightly shifted. It comes to the rest of the State's role in 'appeasing' that is, favoring Muslims. Thus RSS always has claimed that Muslims have been appeased.*

In this manner the article runs and it is easy to assess how slanted and biased each of these statements was.

Virendra Kapoor—Objective

Three articles were selected and all the three were presented to project a balanced view of the whole issue. The article criticized the Congress, BJP and its allies and the Muslim organizations. At the same time the article agreed on all issues raised by the BJP alleging 'pseudo secularism.

Objective

1. The article criticized the cosy relationship that lasted for over 16 months between L.K. Advani and P.V. Narasimha Rao, the Prime Minister, whom Advani once described as the best Prime Minister since Lal Bahadur Shastri.

The following would establish how objectively the author approached on the subject exposing both Congress and the BJP:

While Mr. Rao could expect to make substantial political capital by merely ensuring the status quo in Ayodhya such a course would have proved fatal for the BJP. Thus while Prime Minister might have hoped to keep Lord Rama on the backburner for the entire duration of his five-year term, the BJP, for its fear of losing its newly-acquired appeal in large parts of the country, had to perforce put him up front on the national agenda.

2. The article also highlighted how P.V. Narasimha Rao indulged in politics since the demolition of Babri Masjid to thwart the attempts of his arch rivals Mr. Arjun Singh and S.B. Chavan to unseat him. These compulsions have necessitated Rao to impose ban on RSS, VHP and Bajrang Dal, besides dismissing their duly elected governments in Rajasthan, Madhya Pradesh and Himachal Pradesh.
3. *It is indeed unfortunate that the nation should be expending its energies in this day and age on the genesis of a few stone structures in Ayodhya. But where the secular-progressive elements seem to grievously crr is in their apparent belief that the campaign for a Ram temple can be abandoned mid-way if only they scream the loudest against the BJP-VHP combine. Little do these people seem to realize that in the changed national scene their opposition in effect aids and abets the very forces whom they seek to destroy. (The latest in the progressive-secular tango, viz. the resistance to the singing of the national song, Vande Mataram, in Parliament, is just the kind of issue, which the 'communal-reactionary' BJP loves to exploit. And why not?)*

Criticizing the BJP

Whether the disputed mosque was pulled down in a paroxysm of fundamentalist frenzy or there existed a deeper conspiracy by the zealots of the assorted militant Hindu organizations, Advani alone has to shoulder a major chunk of the blame.

This apart, he even advises the Muslims to reassess their role in society than to depend on certain political groups.

Advising Muslims

1. *Unless Indian Muslims come to temper their angularities in a spirit of give and take with majority community, which necessarily in a democracy must account for a larger say in the decision-making process, there can be no hope for a durable peace in the country. Compromise is the essence of democracy.*

It was only article among the articles of the universe, which boldly came out critically on Muslims attitude towards other religions and advised them to look around.

2. *The short point is that unlike Hinduism, Islam is unhappy to cohabit with other faiths. Muslims may after all pay lip service to multi-culturalism but they believe in exclusivism. It is not a religion, which is comfortable in minority in any given society. Throughout the Islamic world, both modernism and democracy are at discount. It is only on the Indian streets that a Habib Tanvir can get away by doing skits wherein his characters can mouth profanities such as that 'all Brahmins are sons of prostitutes..... And only in India that Lord Rama and Krishna can be called homosexuals in print. And the leaders of the Hindutva party abused as 'scoundrels, liars and rogues.'*
3. *Pause to consider the events around you. Islamic Somalia crushed by the ambitions of two evenly matched warlords has food rushed to it not by the petro-dollar rich Arab world but by the Christian West. Or see how 415 Hams deportees in no-man's land between Israel and Lebanon are able to somehow keep their body and soul together thanks to the Christian, nay, International Red Cross charity. Or consider how Afghan warlords are at each other's throats. Or who is trying to rescue the Bosnian Muslims. Or how the Kurds are on the run from the terror of Saddam* Hussein. Or how Iran and Sudan are seeking to destabilize the rest of the Muslim world. Or even how the Mohajirs are being threatened by the Punjabi Muslims in Pakistan. Or vice versa.

The author finally concludes that the Indian Muslims tried to fall back on the very quality of tolerance of Hindu religion, which they lacked in themselves and did not learn even today when it came to protecting the Babri Masjid.

Bharat Bhushan—Anti-Congress and Slanted

Two articles were basically written and both are Anti-Congress But they admit some of the issues raised by BJP against Congress as 'pseudo secular' as true.

The author held P.V. Narasimha Rao and Congress responsible for the turn of events leading to the demolition of the disputed structure Babri Masjid.

However, he appreciated the steps taken by P.V. Narasimha Rao in banning the RSS, VHP and Bajrang Dal as also dismissing the duly elected BJP governments of Rajasthan, Madhya Pradesh and Himachal Pradesh.

Slanting

Since after much dilly dallying the RSS has been banned now. Mr. Rao will have no option but to follow this up with the dismissal of the BJP governments in Rajasthan, Madhya Pradesh and Himachal Pradesh because they are unlikely to implement the ban order. This many not be bad strategy at all because it will show up the BJP governments as being led by people who are themselves communal.

Anti-Congress

1. *Indeed, it can be argued that Mr. Narasimha Rao's greatest disservice to the Congress party has been his emphasis on the so-called 'consensus' politics. Leave alone the fact that this is a contradiction in terms, it should be clear at least now that this highly marketed and over-subtle magic formula has failed miserably.*
2. *As for the state of the Congress party, it seems in the throes of death. At least after the July 9 incidents in Ayodhya when the BJP and its associates started illegal construction of a temple there, the Congress party should have woken up to the challenge facing the nation and threatening its own survival.*

Even in his second article, the author continued to criticize Congress for its failure to contain BJP's surge ahead.

Over Congress Communalism (agreeing with BJP's allegation of pseudo-secular pursuits).

3. *They thought that communalism could be used to the benefit of the Congress party. Did not Indira Gandhi, therefore, change the public posture of the Congress towards the minorities in her speeches in 1983-84 when she started talking of the rights and privileges of the majority community being suppressed in some places, e.g. Punjab and Kashmir? In November 1983 addressing an Arya Samaj gathering in Ajmer, Indira Gandhi openly said 'our' religion and traditions were under attack and that very year she saw nothing wrong with inaugurating a Bharat Mata temple at Hardwar built by VHP.*

4. *Her son and heir, Rajiv Gandhi, played into the hands of Muslim communalists in the Shah Bhano case and tried to appease the Hindu Communalists by getting the lock on the Ramajanma Bhoomi-Babri Masjid complex opened. As for Narasimha Rao, his antics with the sadhus and the BJP ultimately resulted in the demolition of Babri Masjid...*

Hiranmay Karlekar: Theoretical

Two articles were written and both were purely theoretical yet admits some of the issues raised by the BJP and its combine against Congress and Leftists as true.

Theoretical Statements

Communalism represents the perversion of a religious mass movement which sets out to transform the world and humankind and promises a glorious dawn or life hereafter. It is built-in antithesis of religion and reduces its doctrine of universal love to fragmented love and hatred.

Advise to Counter Communalism

How does a country counter the slide into communalism? Steady economic development and growing prosperity, the creation of climate of rational inquiry which is inimical to the acceptable of blind faith, the growth of individualism which militates against the collectivism of a communal mass movement and the absence of a general feeling of insecurity which spawns neurosis, superstition and dependence on others particularly priests should help. Consider the West, particularly Europe where centuries of intolerance and violence in the name of religion has given way to a secular, humanist outlook.

Favouring BJP's Arguments

1. *The dismissal of the BJP Governments of Himachal Pradesh, Madhya Pradesh and Rajasthan on December 15, following the arrest of leaders like L.K. Advani and the ban on RSS, VHP and Bajrang Dal, the Islamic Sevak Sangh (ISS) and Jamaat-e-Islami Hind, was the second blow to the Constitution. Of the dubious constitutionality, it lent the character of a total confrontation to the political polarization between the BJP and most other parties. It widened the Hindu-Muslim divide by making a large section of Hindus feel that the dismissal represented an attempt by the Congress to 'pander' to the Muslim voter.*

2. *Appeals to the Hindu sentiments by the BJP, RSS and VHP and Bajrang Dal will then find ready response because the reservoir of the Hindu grievance is pretty full. A part of it is accounted for by the memory of Partition and the associated riots. More recently, the Rajiv Gandhi government's legislation to undo the Supreme Court's verdict in the Shah Bano case, obviously enacted under pressure from Muslim fundamentalists, and surrender to the demand to ban The Satanic Verses, have annoyed Hindus; so have the rise of Islamic fundamentalism as a global phenomenon and incidents like the attack on Professor Mushirul Hasan of Jamia Millia Islamia by Muslim Communal elements.*

The author's advice to Congress, BJP and its combine and Muslim organizations is to evolve a consensual space to solve such disputes rather than resorting to the kind of hasty actions that would enhance the divide between the Hindus and Muslims, besides increase the sympathy for BJP and VHP combine.

Avijit Pathak—Pro-BJP

One article was selected and it was written favouring the contentions of BJP-VHP combine, though it condemned the demolition of Babri Masjid.

Favouring BJP

1. *While it is possible to see a genuine concern for communal amity and peace in this kind of argument, the problem is that it has become an official language. It is coming from the Congress establishment whose own record in this regard is by no means satisfactory.*
2. *The ban, the dismissal of the governments – everything has lost its meaning. One can see a very clever politics in it. That is why the confusion. Isn't it a fact that the BJP-RSS-VHP combine has become the only scapegoat?*

The article further criticizes the unprincipled support extended by the Leftist groups for dismissal of duly elected BJP Governments.

S.R. Maheswari: Pro-BJP

One article is selected for the universe and it argued in favour of BJP.

The article discussed at length on the abuse of Article 356 of the Constitution, which empowered the Centre to dismiss the State Governments when the constitutional machinery failed to work.

Anti-Congress

What is more, a hasty dismissal of State Government for alleged non-compliance with the constitutional directions of the Central Government places the latter on a very weak wicket. A State Government duly elected by the people enjoys as much legitimacy as the Central Government.

Asghar Ali Engineer—Anti-BJP and Slanted

One article was written and it was against BJP.

The author claims himself to be *secular* and admires Nehru's *secular* policies which were admittedly Pro-Muslim and were part of BJP and many intellectuals opposition. He claims that singing Vandemataram is unIslamic and feels it should not be applied to Muslims. He too maintains the refrain if Muslims are threatened by the numerically large united majority, it would once again disintegrate the nation. His arguments run in this direction. Here is a classic example of his slanted interpretation.

Slanting

Many scholars maintain that the use of Hindu symbols during the freedom struggle created a sense of alienation in the minds of Muslims and this was one of the contributing factors that strengthened the separatist movement.

Anti-BJP

The textbooks take an extremely partisan view of the past and Rana Sanga, Rana Pratap and Shivaji are projected as heroes and those who fought for liberating Hindus from Muslim tyranny. Even if held sincerely, it is an extremely simplistic view of the Mughal period.

Likewise goes the writing of Asghar Ali Engineer against BJP and its policies in the states where it ruled.

Rajni Kothari—Anti-Congress

One article was written and mostly theoretical but clearly focused against Congress. Accepts one or two issues raised by the BJP-VHP combine.

Anti-Congress

Unfortunately, there developed a near fatal flaw from the way both electoral demography and pluralist culture were interpreted in our unfolding parliamentary democracy, leading to a cultivation first of minorityism and then to majoritism, injecting deep anxiety among the caste Hindus about the whole pluralists model of democracy and national building. It is against this simultaneous promotion of both minoritism and majoritism (both being alien to the core of Indian culture) that the whole of Hindutva has taken place in which I am sorry to say Advani has ridden the crest of both dogma and bigotry.

Favouring BJP

1. *Advani is closer to the ground when he says, 'India is secular because it is predominantly Hindu'.*
2. *The BJP has two choices—first during the movement against the emergency and then its adoption of the formula of 'Gandhian Socialism', embodying a vision of future and humanism—before it became clear that it could emerge as an alternative to the Congress. What was the clear path before the new BJP leadership, the one it had traversed from 1975 to 1989, or the one it went in for 1990, following the admittedly miscalculated and overdone combination of Mandalism and minoritism, together branded as 'secularism' by V.P. Singh, Mulayam Singh Yadav and others?*

Mohan Dharia—Pro-BJP

One article was written and it supported the contentious issues raised by the BJP.

Anti-Congresss

1. *Immediately after the division of the country, Pakistan committed naked aggression and occupied large chunks of territory in Jammu and Kashmir. Instead of repulsing the aggressor, Jawaharlal Nehru's Government, without any reason whatsoever, took the issue to the United Nations, an organization controlled by the Western powers. The result has been a fostering sore and sustained permanent enmity between India and Pakistan and also between Hindus and Muslims in India.*
2. *All political parties—Congress, Janata, Janata Dal and the two*

Communist outfits – some occasion or the other, have indulged communal forces to retain power. This power-oriented approach has been the major cause of the rise of communal and casteist forces in the country. Continuance of Benaras Hindu University and Aligarh Muslim University with religious names or insistence to maintain special status of Jammu and Kashmir under Article 370 of the Constitution, are the result of the same process.

Favouring BJP

It is impossible to preserve secularism and provide any permanent solution by banning certain organizations or dismissing some governments which may perhaps aggravate the situation.

Advice to Muslims and its Leaders

Even though Pakistan was formed on the basis of religion, the rest of India, which had a Hindu majority, resolved to remain a secular country. Unfortunately, most of the Muslims of that time in the country supported the Muslim League and demanded partition without realizing that majority of them will havc to stay in independent India. It would have helped had the Muslim leadership openly accepted this reality and denounced its past action of supporting Muslim League which was responsible for the division of country.

A.M. Khusro – Objective

One article was written and was written in a very objective way.

Objective

In the recent episodes, the leadership of all political parties in this country has been found to be hollow, petty and small minded, preferring short-term gains to long-range benefits and myopic to a forward-looking and broader vision. Self-interest is being placed above party interest and party interest above national interest – leave along international honour or basic human values. With eyes set-on voting in by-election or mid-term polls or end-of-the-term elections, each party is putting principles aside and is taken to abject propaganda and a cheap canvassing of its causes forgetting that parliamentary democracy demands a sensitive and tolerant approach.

Favouring BJP

It is difficult to say whether hauling up of Opposition leaders and the errant politico-religious parties was right or wrong under the circumstances – perhaps, it was right but the dismissal of the BJP governments, duly elected by the people, is probably a grave political error.

Amrik Singh – Anti-Congress

One article was written and was mainly meant to reform the Congress. In the process it agreed with a couple of issues raised by the BJP against Congress too.

Anti-Congress

1. *To look upon the Ayodhya business as a dispute between a mosque and a temple is to completely misread the situation. Owing to the unprincipled policies of the Congress party, the BJP which had been around for almost three quarters of a century was able to outmanoeuvre it in only half a decade.*
2. *Once the gates of the mosque had been unlocked through a swiftly executed maneuvre by the Centre, the BJP was presented with an agenda of work which could not but put up the Congress at an acute disadvantage.*
3. *If the Hindutva onslaught is to be met, the kind of politics played all these years would have to be replaced by new kind of politics. ..... What we need to do is to repudiate those policies of the last four decades where principles were abandoned and vote banks were built and manipulated to suit temporary exigencies and short-term gains.*
4. *The Hindus urge to dominate after a thousand years of ignominy and enslavement needs to be understood....... Had the Congress party which has been in power for four decades not acted only in the interest of the party but also of the country, the situation would have been qualitatively different.*

Jagmohan – Pro-BJP

One article was written and it was purely advisory to Muslims favouring BJP.

The author who was a former Lt. Governor of Delhi writes from his experience of interaction with Muslims how the latter shun their own development and growth in the name of their religious obscurantism by imputing motives to every step taken for their welfare. He cited a classic example of his efforts to relocate the squatters around Idgah and Masjid to Naraina and Mayapuri. The squatters around the Idgah were mostly Hindus and Sikhs who readily agreed to shift to the new place and got high value land at very low price and on installment basis. On the other those who were around Masjid were mostly Muslims and were coaxed by their religious leaders not to relocate and remained there. As a result in a short time the Sikhs and the Hindus who shifted to Naraina and Mayapuri had excellent growth in their economy and healthy living. Their children started studying in good schools and families progressed well on economic path. On the other the Muslims who remained at Masjid itself saw themselves in perennial poverty, ill health and other problems such as intense competition. He bemoaned the lack of spirit among Muslims to see who and what would really help transform their economic development and prosperity.

In his own words, "Ironically, in this *secular* country, one who wanted to preserve the architectural legacy of the two historic mosques, and also gave Muslims an opportunity to carve out a new life of progress and prosperity away from the grooves of dirt and disease, became communal and those who perpetuated their poverty and kept them in virtual serfdom of obscurantist forces, became their 'protectors' and 'well-wishers'."

Amita Abraham—Pro-BJP

One article was written and it favoured BJP on many issues raised by it.

The article tries to dismiss the popular myth around the BJP that due to Rath Yatra or demolition of the Babri Masjid, the BJP could increase its vote bank and prove itself as the sole representative of the Hindu majority. The article says it was only a wishful thinking. It decries the over reaction to the demolition stating that this was no way an increase in fundamentalism.

CH. Hanumantha Rao—Anti-Congress

One article was written and found that one or two issues raised by BJP to be correct.

Anti-Congress

Whether in the pre-independence or in the post-independence period, 'secularism' or equal respect for different faiths has never been preached as an abstract ideal, in isolation from other secular issues.

The article suggests that given the economic development and reforms, removal of poverty and improved education should curb the unemployment and youth being tempted towards non-secular movements.

K.R. Malkani—Pro-BJP

Two articles were taken and both were written highlighting the BJP's contentions how Congress and Leftist groups indulged in non-secular policies pretending to be secular. It also sums up the Muslims attitude to lead a crab-life and freely integrating with the Hindus on many issues.

Statistical Analysis

When the Edit Page Articles written by different authors have been analyzed against the 18 contentions raised by the BJP, about 10 authors have identified 5 issues, such as Appeasement politics, Vote bank politics, Banning of Satanic Verses, Reversing Shah Bhano Judgment, Opening the gates of Babri Masjid for Muslims, have been accepted as truly contentious and have been cause of the drifting of the situation to such a pass where it became difficult to determine who was *secular* since independence.

As many as 9 authors believed that, besides other issues already stated, issues like opening of Ram Temple Gates for Shilanyas and continuance of Article 370 of Jammu and Kashmir, have been contentious as alleged by the BJP and its combine. As such total 7 issues have been identified as crucial in holding all the political parties responsible, especially Congress-Left and National Front, for rendering the *secular* character of the state vague.

About 4 authors, namely G.M. Telang (GMT), Achin Vanaik (AV), Bharat Bhushan (BB) and Asghar Ali Engineer (AAE) had written articles consisting of slanted statements that lacked in balance of approach and equal treatment to the contending issues. The slanted statements are identified and given in italicized paragraphs against each author's statements.

Analysis of Non-Edit Page Articles Written by Politicians and Intellectuals

L.K. Advani—Pro-BJP

Two articles were written and both were defending the BJP though they expressed regret over the demolition of the Babri Masjid.

The articles narrated clearly how the issue of Ayodhya Ram Temple became crucial for the BJP in the wake of Mandal and Minority issue raised by V.P. Singh in a bid to out wit Mulayam Singh and Devi Lal. Advani also traced how *pseudo secularism* was pursued for over 4 decades by the Congress and the successive governments, which necessitated the BJP and VHP, combine to identify an issue that would unify the Hindus and consolidate them to oppose the political appeasement. As such Ram Temple and Ayodhya issue became quite handy for the BJP to expose the *pseudo secular* forces.

K. Govindan Kutty—Anti-Left

One article was written to fully expose the double standards maintained by the Leftists groups in opposing and favoring the article 356–dismissing the duly elected state governments – to suit their convenience and gain politically.

Arun Nehru—Pro-BJP

One article was written and it defended the BJP's contention that Congress and National Front indulged in blatant appeasement and vote bank politics.

The article clearly traced out the events that led to BJP's taking up Ayodhya issue to expose the *pseudo secularism* pursued by the Congress, Left and National Front political groups. In many aspects of stating the facts, the article gains credence by reentering the facts cited by L.K. Advani and other top BJP-VHP combine leaders.

Soli Sorabjee—Anti-Congress

One article was written and it opposed the Congress action of dismissing the State Governments of BJP under Article 356 of the constitution in the aftermath of demolition of Babri Masjid.

The article repeats almost similar arguments of K. Govindan Kutty's exposing the hollowness of the Left Groups in so far use of Article 356 of the Constitution in dismissing the duly elected State Governments.

Nawab Zafar Jung—Anti-BJP Slanted

One article was written and it condemned the demolition of Babri Masjid by BJP-VHP combine.

The article condemns the atrocities perpetrated on the Muslim girls in the riots in Surat and Ahemdabad in the BJP ruled state. It further condemned the role of BJP and VHP combine insofar the incident of demolition of Babri Masjid. It also alleged that the idols were placed inside the Masjid stealthily on December 21, 1949. Therefore, it would not lose its status of Masjid as claimed by Advani in his article published in *Indian Express* on December 27, 1992.

Slanted

The article contains some slanted statements. It does not speak of many issues raised against Muslims and Islam as to their religious intolerance and keeping their faiths above the law of the land. Nor does he speak about the appeasement politics indulged in by the Congress and Leftists groups, besides National Front leaders like V.P. Singh, Mulayam Singh Yadav.

All the statements of slanting notwithstanding, he had some objective statements also to inform his readers.

Objective

Yet the author was one rarely found to state openly that "Muslim is first an Indian and last an Indian."

Irfan Habib—Anti-BJP Slanted*

One article was written and was against BJP.

The article calls for people to look into BJP's issues with reason while making a number of slanted statements both against the media and intellectuals, some of which are selected for the study here.

**Slanted*

> *The 'Hindutva' upsurge masterminded by the BJP-Sangh Parivar does not stem from any positive programme of reform or of national growth and development, but is purely negative in content. Its centerpiece has been the charge that the Muslims have been 'appeased' by the Indian (pseudo-secular) state since Independence, the appeasement making for a provocative 'minorityism' at the expense of the Hindus. Many sages in our press and among politicians have tended, during the last few years, to accept the basic premises of the BJP campaigners and have begun to recommend a parallel pursuit of the same cause by the ruling party.*

Countering BJP (Slanting the BJP's Statement)

1. *The principal assumption that the BJP has put forward is that the Muslims are not part of the Indian nation. They are, in culture and thought, 'foreigners'. There is, of course, no concern with history here; no migration took place in medieval Muslim population in the subcontinent. It is, therefore, absurd to say that Muslims have not 'adapted' themselves to India.*
2. *As for the case of 'minorityism' of the Indian State, the instance most loudly cited in Parliament's refusal to interfere with Muslim Personal Law, and its reversal of the Shah Bano Judgment of the Supreme Court. Clearly, the securing of full rights to women, through equality in inheritance and ban on bigamy, must be an indispensable part of the democratic movement in India; and the reversal of the Supreme Court judgment, despite strong opposition from Muslim reformers, was manifestly wrong.*

Though the author tried to counter the BJP's allegation of Muslims extraterritorial loyalties, his reply was far from being the apt reply to the BJP in point 1. But his admission of BJP's allegation of 'appeasement' of Muslims indulged in by Congress by reversing judgment in Shah Bano case is a step forward in coming into an objective self-assessment mode. To that extent it is balanced approach in the entire article.

Krishna Mahajan – Pro-BJP

One article was written and it defends the BJP-VHP combine's contention for Ram Temple.

One sensational article on Judicial reporting stating that Indian Constitution in its original accepted form by the Constituent Assembly conceded that Lord Rama was one among the 22 leading luminaries that India can boast of. In this way it defends the BJP-VHP combine's contention that Ram Temple in Ayodhya is a nation's requirement and need.

The article quotes the judgment of HN Tilhari and AN Gupta on the objection raised by the Muslim bodies in allowing darshan of Ram idols located in the demolished Babri structure.

The judges gave a lengthy interpretation in their 63 pages judgment for allowing darshan to Lord Rama's idols and argued strongly that Constituent Assembly agreed Lord Ram as our national hero and hence a temple for him is in the fitness of the things where Muslims had to act with large heartedness.

P. Parameswaran – Pro-BJP

One article was written and it was completely favoring the BJP–VHP combine demand for a Ram Temple.

The article explained why Ram Temple is necessary. The author being the Vice-President of Vivekananda Rock Memorial, Kanya Kurmari stongly argued how temples like Ram Temple would epitomize the glory of ancient Indian culture and its heritage.

Salman Kursheed – Anti-BJP Slanted*

One article was written and its main import was anti-BJP. It makes a number of slanted statements in its articulation of arguments.

**Slanted*

'Appeasement' of minorities is cited as the reason of a rising wave of Hindutva. This would make sense if the minorities have been given something at the cost of the majority. If they got a share of the cake reserved for the majority one could understand the cause of complaint. If the minorities wish to eat their share of the cake in a particular way it cannot be called 'appeasement'.

Likewise the article goes in a very superficial way in countering the deep and highly informed criticism of the BJP on this issue and other issues.

Surprisingly the author tries to speak about the greatness of Hinduism and Lord Ram's greatness and tries to fall back on the 'secular' minded Hindu approach. At the same time he wouldn't speak whether Islam and Muslims had such record of 'tolerance', nor did he try to substantiate the greatness of Islam in tolerating the others faith. The author also adds that the term 'secular' became more self-conscious and fell the defense.

On Confusing Import of the Term 'Secular'

We began using words like 'secularism' at a time when everybody knew or could understand what that word meant. We have got to a point in time when it is no longer clear what it meant.

R.L.M. Patil—Pro BJP

One article was written and it was completely in defense of the arguments of BJP and VHP Combine.

The article tries to explode the popular myth in the claims of the Congress, Leftists and National Front leaders that they are *secular* and that 'BJP' alone is 'communal'.

On Secularism

1. Secularism is not ingrained in the hearts and minds of millions and millions of the people of India whereas religion is. A fake superimposition of a non-workable, non-popular or a pseudo concept of secularism won't work in this country or in any other.
2. It may not be too much off the mark to say that for the Congress-led country, to be *secular* means to appease the minority especially the Muslim. On the converse, to denigrate the self, that is the Hindu, is the proof of *secularism*. This approach is neither scientific nor emotionally sound, for nearly a thousand years India has lived under the Hindu, Muslim and the Christian rulers—without the operative principle of *secularism*.

Anti-Congress

> *The Congressmen's belief in 'secularism' is not deep or complete. They say 'secular' but do communal things. .....When power came into their own hands they started a policy of appeasement of the Muslims and other minorities as though they had real love for them.*

Advice to the Nation

What happened at Ayodhya was in a sense inevitable and ought to open our eyes to the ground reality. What the Congress Government and the leftist intellectuals were indulging in so far was an ethereal dream. It only ended up in frustration for the Hindus and false security for the Muslims. The razing of Babri Masjid is unfortunate but it now becomes a historic turning point inasmuch as it busted the false god of secularism is preached by the Congressmen. A true Hindu-Mulsim-Christian affinity can be raised only on the basis of a true foundation of Gandhiji's concept of 'Sarva Dharma Samabhava' and not on the false foundation of 'dharma nirpekshata'.

M.M Sankhdher—Pro-BJP

One article was written and was defending BJP's contentious issues.

The article makes a balanced effort to convince both Muslims and the Hindus to make a step forward in normalizing their relationships by understanding mutual feelings.

J. Swaminathan—Anti-BJP *Slanted

One article was written and was against BJP-VHP combine.

The article runs on highly slanted statements a couple of which were given below:

**Slanted*

1. This concept of secularism sits well on the shoulders of the Indian people, especially on those of the majority community, the Hindus.
2. The pulling down of the Babri Masjid by a tightly knit organized band of revanchists from the majority community has therefore come as a profound shock. It is not only an attack on behalf of a particular community, but a gauntlet thrown at constitutional authority and an insult offered to the Hindu ethos itself.

Likewise the article tries to depend on the broadminded and open minded character of Hindus but does not speak a single word on the alleged intolerance of Muslims and Islam towards other religions.

K.S. Duggal—Anti-BJP

One article was written and it was anti-BJP in tone.

The author advises the BJP to act in the spirit of the Hindu ethos though the author too believes that the Ram temple is a prerequisite at Ayodhya to fulfill the dream of the Hindus.

Swapan Dasgupta—Objective

One article was written and it made an objective approach towards the contentious issues raised by the BJP-VHP combine.

Statistical Analysis

Out of 15 articles written by 14 authors, of whom two to three were politicians, three to four were legal experts and nearly 3 authors were Muslims, seven articles were Pro-BJP and five articles were Anti-BJP. It means the authors have agreed about 46 per cent of the contentious issues raised. Similarly about 33 per cent issues were considered as incorrect.

Out of the 18 issues raised as contentious by the BJP, about two issues related to Vote bank and Appeasement were agreed to be true (as alleged by the BJP) by as many as 11 authors. Nearly 8 authors agreed that Opening of Babri Majdi Gates for Muslims and Ram Temple for Hindus by Congress were also contentious as alleged by the BJP -VHP combine.

Analysis of Articles of Sunday Magazine

About 7 articles were taken as the sample most of which were written by Talveen Singh, a regular columnist of Indian Express Sunday Magazine, Rajee Suri, Bhasker Roy and Goutam Sen. Almost all of them were written in anti-BJP diction.

Talveen Singh—Anti-BJP

She has written total 3 articles all of which are arrayed against BJP-VHP combine though she was occasionally agreeing with the contentious issues raised by the BJP.

The author condemns the BJP-VHP role in the demolition of Babri Masjid and describes them as pseudo-fascists. At the same time she nearly agrees with the contentions of the BJP-VHP combine on their allegation of other political groups pursuing pseudo-secularism. Her approach looks quite balanced as far as these issues are concerned but short of demolishing the Babri Masjid, she appreciated the vituperous attack mounted by L.K. Advani against opposition for their alleged communal character and 'pseudo secular' policies including appeasement of minorities.

Favouring BJP's Contentions

1. Secular (by this I mean non-religious) parties, thanks mainly to their own idiocies, were knocked out and almost finished

by the simple argument that secularism could not be synonym for minority communalism, which it had clearly become.

2. She did not agree with the dismissal of BJP governments in Madhya Pradesh, Rajasthan and Himachal Pradesh.

Anti-BJP

For a start, whatever the faults of pseudo-secularism, it is infinitely less dangerous than pseudo-fascism, which is what we are being offered by our Hindu-minded friends.

Real Secularism Defined by the Author

1. For, much as the BJP would have us believe the opposite, there is such a thing as real secularism.
2. It means the state conduct its affairs by keeping priests out of them and keeping itself out of religion. In the context of modern India it would mean that the Government would not involve itself in trying to break or build temples or mosques.

M.M. Shankdher—Anti-BJP

One article was written and it was Anti-BJP since the article was a review of the book of Saeed Naqvi – "Reflection of an Indian Muslim."

The review made a new point of the author of the book. The author of the book opined that the Muslims in the South are comparatively economically better off than the Muslims of the North. He was of the opinion that to some extent this was responsible for the religious bigotry of the North Muslims than the South.

Rajee Suri : Anti-BJP

One article was written and it was written to mock the BJP for its one-sided effort to highlight Ayodhya issue whereas many more temples are in a dilapidated condition.

Bhasker Roy—Anti-BJP

One article was written and it was against BJP–RSS combine.

It detailed the RSS growth since independence and how it operated with the other cultural organizations such as VHP, Bajrang Dal for the growth of Sangh Pariwar.

Goutam Sen: Anti-BJP

One article was written but it meant totally against BJP but it agrees with the BJP on one or two contentious issues related to 'pseudo secularism'.

Statistical Analysis

1. All articles exhibited marked anti-BJP stand and fear of nation slipping into fundamentalism flaunted by the Hindu fundamentalist forces such as VHP, RSS and Bajrang Dal.
2. All articles at least agreed on half-a-dozen issues raised by the BJP as contentious and pseudo-secular politics of the Congress and Leftist groups including Janata Dal.
3. Writers like Talveen Singh clearly came out openly stating there is a need to change the present understanding of *secularism* and even suggested rapid economic development as a panacea for weaning away the national youth from slipping into the religious fanatism unleashed by the BJP-VHP combine.
4. However, most of the articles lacked the balanced approach to speak against the backwardness in Muslims and their religious bigotry, which again reflected a kind of appeasement of Muslims by the authors themselves who blamed the political parties for appeasement and minoritism.

6

Portrayal of Secularism in the Media: Unit Analysis and Item Analysis of the Hindu

Analysis of the Editorials of *The Hindu*

In all about 13 Editorials have been selected to constitute the universe of the sample. They indeed became the representative sample of *The Hindu* by virtue of the fact that the names of the Editors who had drafted the Editorials on a given day were not known and that they were drafted by various Editors of the combined Editorial College of the Hindu representing the national character of the Press.

A critical analysis of these editorials, of which one was before the demolition of Babri Masjid on December 6, 1992, and the rest were consecutively afterwards for a month, reveals that the Editorials written both before and after clearly showed strong signs of anti-BJP stance and Pro-Congress on the following issues, which indeed constituted the core content of the Editorials.

The following is the break up of number of articles, which suggest a clear polarization of *The Hindu* towards Congress:

(i)	Anti BJP or Pro-Congress	:	11(79%)
(ii)	Anti-Congress	:	1 (07%)
(iii)	Objective	:	2 (14%)
(iv)	Pro-BJP	:	0

The following list of points favoring Congress and castigating the BJP and its cultural allies VHP, RSS and Bajrang Dal would clearly testify to the polarization of Press on the political lines.

Anti-BJP or Pro-Congress

1. Sending the troops into Uttar Pradesh on the eve of proposed *kar seva* despite the opposition of the Kalyan Singh's government and exhorting the need to intervene further should the matters go beyond the professed claims of the BJP and its allies such as VHP, RSS and Bajrang Dal that *kar seva* would be mere ritual and symbolic (Pull back from the brink: December 5, 1992).
2. Suggesting the arrest of the leaders of the BJP and its allies VHP, RSS and Bajrang Dal and supporting the arrest of these leaders subsequently all through (Tragic Aftermath: December 8, 1992; Tragic Refrain: December 10, 1992; Re-establishing the fundamental values: December 12, 1992).
3. Supporting the Ban on all Cultural organizations espousing the religious cause of their sects—VHP, RSS and Bajrang Dal (Re-establishing the fundamental values: December 12, 1992; The aftermath: December 15, 1992).
4. Supporting the dismissal of the State Governments of Madhya Pradesh, Rajasthan and Himachal Pradesh, besides Uttar Pradesh. (Inevitable: December 17, 1992).
5. Appreciating the Defeat of the Motion of No-Confidence against Mr. P.V. Narasimha Rao Government (BJP Remains Isolated: December 23, 1992).
6. Holding BJP responsible for the impasse in the Parliament and consequent adjournment for a week sans discussion (Disrupting the Parliament: December 18, 1992).

Opposing Congress

1. Not supported the Presidential reference to Supreme Court under article 143 or 138 as it amounted to giving legal sanctity to the claims of the VHP, RSS and Bajrang Dal (Disturbing Implications: January 9, 1993).
2. Holding Rao's Government and Congress in general accountable for allowing the situation to drift to a pass leading to the destruction of the Babri Masjid (Tragic Aftermath: December 8, 1992).
3. Not appreciated allowing Darshan of Ram Lala idols installed at the site of destruction of the Babri Masjid by devout Hindus (Legitimizing Vandalism: December 29, 1992).

Favouring IUML (Indian Union of Muslim League)

Not criticizing the Congress for its alleged electoral alliances with IUML both in Kerala and West Bengal, Assam, etc., while claiming itself to be a *secular* party.

Neutral Stand

Castigating the *secular* credentials of all non-BJP political parties including Congress, Janata Dal, V. P. Singh National Democratic

Table-6.1
Treatment of Editorials Taken for Analysis
The Hindu, December, 1992–January 1993

Sl. No.	*Date of the Editorial*	*Title of the Editorial*	*Remarks*
1.	Dec 5, 92	Pull Back from the Brink	Anti-BJP
2.	Dec 7, 92	Unforgivable	Anti-BJP
3.	Dec 8, 92	Tragic Aftermath	Anti-BJP
4.	Dec 10, 92	Tragic Refrain	Anti-BJP
5.	Dec 12, 92	Reestablishing Fundamental Values	Anti-BJP
6.	Dec 15, 92	The Aftermath	Anti-BJP
7.	Dec 16, 92	The Muslim League Stays	Anti BJP & Pro-Muslim
8.	Dec 17, 92	Inevitable	Anti-BJP
9.	Dec 18, 92	Disrupting Parliament	Anti-BJP
10.	Dec 23, 92	BJP Remains Isolated	Anti-BJP
11.	Dec 29, 92	Legitimizing vandalism	Anti-BJP
12.	Dec 30, 92	The New Relevance of Vivekananda	Teaching Tolerance to Hindus but not a word to Muslims on this important issue.
13.	Jan 9, 93	Disturbing Implications	Opposing Congress for letting Darshan and referring to Supreme Court on the existence of temple where Babri Masjid stood.

Out of 13 the following is the break-up of number of articles:

(i)	Anti-BJP or Pro-Congress	:	11
(ii)	Anti-Congress	:	1
(iii)	Advisory and neutral categories	:	2
(iv)	Pro-BJP	:	0

Figure 6.1 : Analysis of Treatment of Editorials in the Hindu, Dec. 1992 to Jan. 1993

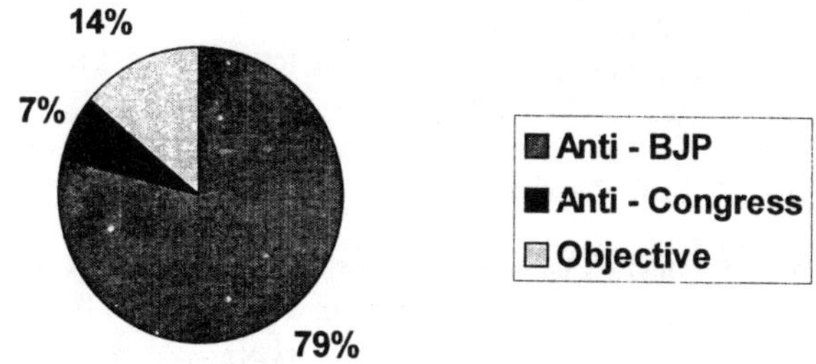

Figure 6.2 : Analysis of Treatment of Editorials in the Hindu, Dec. 1992 to Jan. 1993

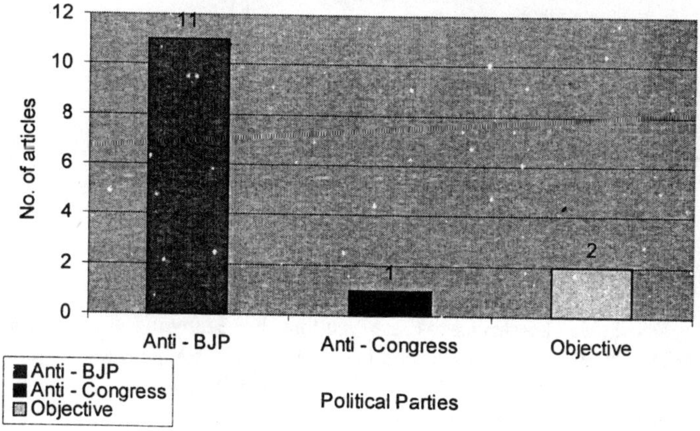

Table–6.2

Treatment of Edit Page Articles—The Hindu, December 1992-January 1993

Sl. No.	*Date*	*Title of Edit Page Article*	*Author's Name*	*Remarks*
1.	Dec 8, 92	The BJP's hour of reckoning	Prem Shankar Jha (PSJ)	Pro-Cong
2.	Dec 9, 92	A Noble dream Shattered	Hasan Suroor(HS)	Pro-JD
3.	Dec 10, 92	A Barbarity and Otiosity	VR Krishna Iyer (VRK)	Anti-BJP

(Contd.)

Sl. No.	*Date*	*Title of Edit Page Article*	*Author's Name*	*Remarks*
4.	Dec 12, 92	Ayodhya and Structural Adjustment	PV Indiresan (PVI)	Objective
5.	Dec 14, 92	The Parties after the trauma	KK Katyal (KKK)	Pro-Cong
6.	Dec 15, 92	Test for Secular Forces	Asghar Ali Engineer (AAE)	Anti-BJP
7.	Dec 16, 92	Urdu Press on Aydhya	Suneet Vir Singh (SVS)	Pro-JD
8.	Dec 16, 92	The Task before the nation	KN Panikkar (KNP)	Anti-BJP
9.	Dec 17, 92	The beginning of a long war	Prem Shankar Jha (PSJ)	Pro-Cong
10.	Dec 17, 92	Confusion in the Hindi Press	Suneet Vir Singh (SVS)	Pro-JD
11.	Dec 19, 92	Ayodhya and Macro Politics	Pran Chopra (PC)	Pro-BJP
12.	Dec 19, 92	Can We Swim or must we sink	Sudhanshu Ranade (SR)	Objective
13.	Dec 21, 92	Clearer Lines and unclear Future	KK Katyal (KKK)	Pro-Cong
14.	Dec 21, 92	Cong (I) keep its promises	M.S. Prabhakara (MSP)	Anti-Cong
15.	Dec 22, 92	Fascistic Pseudo-Hinduism	Sitaram Yechury (SY)	Anti-BJP
16.	Dec 22, 92	Ayodhya; the rule of the courts	HR Khanna (HRK)	Objective
17.	Dec 23, 92	Collapse of Centrist Forces	Prem Shankar Jha (PSJ)	Pro-Cong
18.	Dec 24, 92	Disservice to Press Freedom	Era Sezhyan (ES)	Anti-BJP
19.	Dec 24, 92	Police and the Bombay Riots	Mahesh Vijapurkar (MV)	Objective
20.	Dec 29, 92	Ayodhya and the Indian State	CP Bhambhri (CPB)	Objective
21.	Dec 29, 92	Why were Bombay riots so fierce?	Kalpana Sharma (KS)	Objective
22.	Dec 30, 92	Can the secular center revive?	Prem Shankar Jha (PSJ)	Pro-Cong
23.	Jan 1, 93	Varied Response to Ayhodhya	KK Katyal (KKK)	Pro-Cong
24.	Jan 4, 93	Dec 6 and after	KK Katyal (KKK)	Pro-Cong
25.	Jan 13, 93	The Choice is Yours, Mr. Advani	Prem Shankar Jha (PSJ)	Pro-Cong
26.	–	Make or break for the Congress	Prem Shankar Jha (PSJ)	Pro-Cong
27.	–	Inept Handling of a Sensitive issue	Muchikund Debey (MD)	Pro-Cong

Pro-Cong = 11; Anti-BJP = 5; Pro-JD = 3; Anti-Cong = 1; Objective = 6; Pro-BJP = 1.

Figure 6.3 : Analysis of Treatment of Edit Page Articles— The Hindu, Dec. 1992 to Jan. 1993

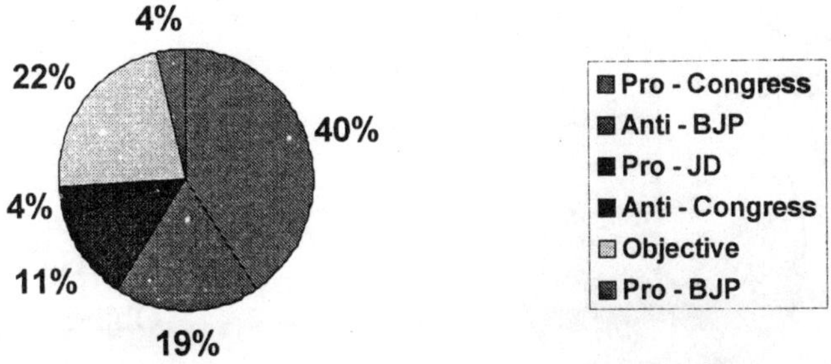

Figure 6.4 : Analysis of Treatment of Edit Page Articles—The Hindu, Dec. 1992 to Jan. 1993

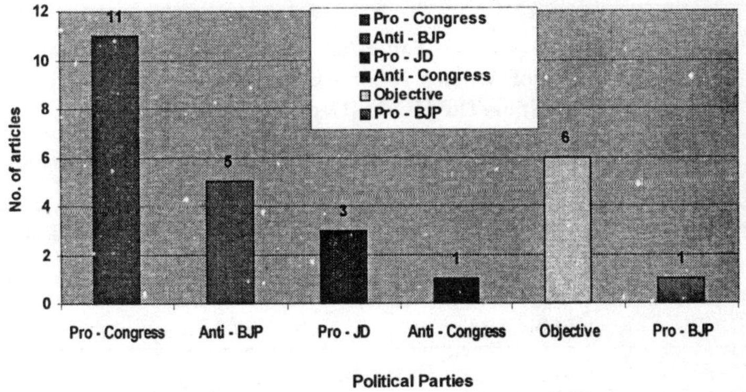

Table–6.3

Treatment of Press Statements and Special Contributions Taken for Analysis – Non-Edit Page–The Hindu, Dec 1992–Jan, 1993.

Sl. No.	*Date*	*Title*	*Author*	*Remarks*
1.	Oct 6, 92	Rewriting History – the BJP Way	News Bureau	Anti-BJP
2.	Dec 19, 92	Interesting finds from debris, say experts	News Bureau	Anti-BJP
3.	Dec 1, 92	Vajpayee calls for equality of religions	News Bureau	Objective
4.	Dec 14, 92	It was a countdown for a 'coup'	News Bureau	Anti-BJP
5.	Dec 8, 92	Crucial days for the nation	Prem Shankar Jha	Anti-BJP

Figure 6.5 : Analysis of Treatment of Press Statements and Special Contributions—Non-Edit Page Articles–The Hindu, Dec. 1992 to Jan. 1993

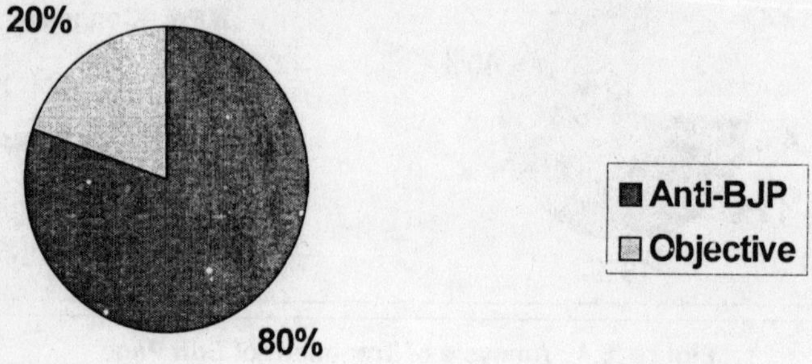

Table–6.4
Treatment of Articles Taken for Analysis – Sunday Magazine – The Hindu, Dec. 1992-Jan. 1993

Sl. No.	*Date*	*Title*	*Author*	*Remarks*
1.	Dec 6, 92	Communalism: A view from the South	Saeed Naqvi	Objective
2.	Dec 13, 92	We have met the enemy, and he is us	Madhu Limaye	Anti-BJP

Table–5
Treatment of Interviews Taken for Analysis – The Hindu Dec. 1992-Jan. 1993

Sl. No.	*Date*	*Title*	*Interviews*	*Remarks*
1.	Dec 11, 92	We Should be firm in dealing with Communal Elements	Arjun Singh	Anti-BJP
2.	Dec 18, 92	Joint Front should involve all secular forces	Har Kishen Singh Surjeet	Anti-BJP
3.	Dec 25, 92	Rao has lost all credibility	Chandrasekar	Anti-BJP
4.	Dec 28, 92	Hindu Militancy will lead to bloodshed	VP Singh	Anti-BJP
5.	....	BJP not for a communal Divide	Vajpayee	Pro-BJP

Table-6.6

Analysis of Agreement and Disagreement of the Editorials of Indian Express and The Hindu on Theoretical Issues Dec. 1992-Jan. 1993

S. No.	*Theoretical Issues*	*Editorial Indian Express*	*Editorial The Hindu*
1.	Western Secular Model (US and European Model)	@	@
2.	(Undefined) Secular model of Indian Constitution with strong Pro-minority inclination	@	+
3.	All religions as equal and removal of pro-minority inclination in Constitution	@	@
4.	Secular Model from Atheistic and Agnostic schools		
5.	Anti-Hindu Unity but protect Pro-minority inclinations		

\+ Indicates the issues dealt with by the concerned author directly or implicitly.

@ Not spoken on the issue but chose to speak on other issues like banning the RSS. VHP etc., and dismissal of BJP Governments in Rajasthan, MP and Himachal Pradesh.

Table-6.7

Analysis of the Political Issues Discussed by Number of Authors—Edit Page Articles-The Hindu, Dec. 1992-Jan. 1993

Sl. No.	*Political Issues*	*PSJ*	*HS*	*VRK*	*PVI*
1.	Appeasement of Minorities by the Congress and other political groups	+	@	@	+
2.	Vote bank politics for garnering Minorities' Votes during elections-Congress, Left and other Groups	+	@	@	+
3.	Implementation of Uniform Civil Code	+	@	@	+
4.	Building up Consensus on disputed structures and shrines	+	@	@	@
5.	On the Role and Character of RSS and VHP (Communal)	+	+	@	+
6.	On the Communal Riots-Role of Congress (Communal)	@		@	+

(Contd.)

Sl. No.	Political Issues	PSJ	HS	VRK	PVI
7.	On the Communal Riots-Role of BJP, RSS and VHP	+	@	@	+
8.	On Banning Satanic Verses of Salman Rushdie-Rajiv Congress	+	@	@	@
9.	On Reversing Shah Bano Judgment of Supreme Court-Rajiv Congess (Vote Bank)	+	@	@	@
10.	On Opening the Gates of Babri Masjid-Appeasing Muslims to do prayers at Mosque—Rajiv Congress (Vote Bank)	+	@	@	@
11.	On Opening the Gates of Ram Lala temple appeasing Hindus and performing Shilanyas-Rajiv Congress (Vote Bank)	+	@	@	@
12.	On BJP's demand for Scrapping Article 370 on Jammu and Kashmir	+	@	@	@
13.	On Political Alliances and Clandestine Supports from Indian Muslim League and Other Communal Bodies-Congress and other political groups	+	@	@	+
14.	On the demand of BJP to check Illegal Migrations and Changing Demographic Distributions	+	@	@	@
15.	On Lack of population control, prevalence of polygamy among Muslims	@	@	@	@
16.	Ban on Cow Slaughter	@	@	@	@
17.	On the Muslims Education in Madarsas	@	@	@	@
18.	On the BJP's demand to check the Conversions to Islam and Christianity-Silence of Congress and other political groups	@	@	@	@

\+ Indicates the issues dealt with by the concerned author directly or implicitly.

@ Not spoken on the issue but chose to speak on other issues like banning the RSS, VHP etc. and dismissal of BJP Governments in Rajasthan, MP and Himachal Pradesh.

Front for having aligned themselves with the BJP, knowing fully its affiliations with the RSS, VHP and Bajrang Dal (Re-establishing the fundamental values: December 12, 1992).

Table-6.8

Analysis of the Political Issues Discussed by Number of Authors—Edit Page Articles-The Hindu, Dec. 1992-Jan. 1993

Sl. No.	*Political Issues*	*KKK*	*AAE*	*SVS*	*KNP*
1.	Appeasement of Minorities by the Congress and other political groups	+	+	+	@
2.	Vote bank politics for garnering Minorities' Votes during elections—Congress, Left and other Groups	+	@	+	@
3.	Implementation of Uniform Civil Code	+	@	@	@
4.	Building up Consensus on disputed structures and shrines	@	+	+	@
5.	On the Role and Character of RSS and VHP (Communal)	+	+	+	@
6.	On the Communal Riots—Role of Congress (Communal)	+	@	+	@
7.	On the Communal Riots—Role of BJP, RSS and VHP	@	+	+	@
8.	On Banning Satanic Verses of Salman Rushdie-Rajiv Congrcss	@		@	@
9.	On Reversing Shah Bano Judgment of Supreme Court—Rajiv Congess (Vote Bank)	+	+	@	@
10.	On Opening the Gates of Babri Masjid-Appeasing Muslims to do prayers at Mosque—Rajiv Congress (Vote Bank)	+	+	@	@
11.	On Opening the Gates of Ram Lala temple appeasing Hindus and performing Shilanyas-Rajiv Congress (Vote Bank)	+	+	@	@
12.	On BJP's demand for Scrapping Article 370 on Jammu and Kashmir	@	@	@	@
13.	On Political Alliances and Clandestine Supports from Indian Muslim League and Other Communal Bodies—Congress and other political groups	+	+	@	@
14.	On the demand of BJP to check Illegal Migrations and Changing Demographic Distributions	@	@	@	@
15.	On Lack of population control, prevalence of polygamy among Muslims	@	@	@	@
16.	Ban on Cow Slaughter	@	@	@	@

(Contd.)

Sl. No.	Political Issues	KKK	AAE	SVS	KNP
17.	On the Muslims Education in Madarsas	@	@	@	@
18.	On the BJP's demand to check the Conversions to Islam and Christianity – Silence of Congress and other political groups	@	@	@	@

\+ Indicates the issues dealt with by the concerned author directly or implicitly.

@ Not spoken on the issue but chose to speak on other issues like banning the RSS. VHP etc., and dismissal of BJP Governments in Rajasthan, MP and Himachal Pradesh.

Table–6.9

Analysis of the Political Issues Discussed by Number of Authors – Edit Page Articles–The Hindu, Dec. 1992 –Jan. 1993

Sl. No.	Political Issues	PC	SR	MSP	SY
1.	Appeasement of Minorities by the Congress and other political groups	@	@	+	@
2.	Vote bank politics for garnering Minorities' Votes during elections – Congress, Left and other Groups	@	@	+	@
3.	Implementation of Uniform Civil Code	@	@	+	@
4.	Building up Consensus on disputed structures and shrines	@	@	+	@
5.	On the Role and Character of RSS and VHP (Communal)	@	@	+	+
6.	On the Communal Riots – Role of Congress (Communal)	@	@	@	@
7.	On the Communal Riots – Role of BJP, RSS and VHP	@	@	@	@
8.	On Banning Satanic Verses of Salman Rushdie-Rajiv Congress	@	@	@	@
9.	On Reversing Shah Bano Judgment of Supreme Court- Rajiv Congress (Vote Bank)	@	@	@	@
10.	On Opening the Gates of Babri Masjid-Appeasing Muslims to do prayers at Mosque – Rajiv Congress (Vote Bank)	@	@	+	@
11.	On Opening the Gates of Ram Lala temple appeasing Hindus and performing Shilanyas-Rajiv Congress (Vote Bank)	@	@	+	@

(Contd.)

Sl. No.	Political Issues	PC	SR	MSP	SY
12.	On BJP's demand for Scrapping Article 370 on Jammu and Kashmir	@	@	@	@
13.	On Political Alliances and Clandestine Supports from Indian Muslim League and Other Communal Bodies—Congress and other political groups	@	@	@	@
14.	On the demand of BJP to check Illegal Migrations and Changing Demographic Distributions	@	@	@	@
15.	On Lack of population control, prevalence of polygamy among Muslims	@	@	@	@
16.	Ban on Cow Slaughter	@	@	@	@
17.	On the Muslims Education in Madarsas	@	@	@	@
18.	On the BJP's demand to check the Conversions to Islam and Christianity—Silence of Congress and other political groups	@	@	@	@

+ Indicates the issues dealt with by the concerned author directly or implicitly.

@ Not spoken on the issue but chose to speak on other issues like banning the RSS. VHP etc., and dismissal of BJP Governments in Rajasthan, MP and Himachal Pradesh.

Table–6.10

Analysis of the Political Issues Discussed by Number of Authors—Edit Page Articles—The Hindu, Dec. 1992-Jan. 1993

Sl. No.	Political Issues	HK	ES	MV	CPB
1.	Appeasement of Minorities by the Congress and other political groups	@	@	@	+
2.	Vote bank politics for garnering Minorities' Votes during elections—Congress, Left and other Groups	@	@	@	+
3.	Implementation of Uniform Civil Code	@	@	@	@
4.	Building up Consensus on disputed structures and shrines	+	+	@	+
5.	On the Role and Character of RSS and VHP (Communal)	@	@	@	+
6.	On the Communal Riots—Role of Congress (Communal)	@	@	@	+
7.	On the Communal Riots—Role of BJP, RSS and VHP	@	@	@	+

(Contd.)

Sl. No.	Political Issues	HK	ES	MV	CPB
8.	On Banning Satanic Verses of Salman Rushdie-Rajiv Congress	@	@	@	@
9.	On Reversing Shah Bano Judgment of Supreme Court-Rajiv Congress (Vote Bank)	@	@	@	@
10.	On Opening the Gates of Babri Masjid-Appeasing Muslims to do prayers at Mosque – Rajiv Congress (Vote Bank)	@	@	@	@
11.	On Opening the Gates of Ram Lala temple appeasing Hindus and performing Shilanyas-Rajiv Congress (Vote Bank)	@	@	@	@
12.	On BJP's demand for Scrapping Article 370 on Jammu and Kashmir	@	@	@	@
13.	On Political Alliances and Clandestine Supports from Indian Muslim League and Other Communal Bodies – Congress and other political groups	@	@	@	@
14.	On the demand of BJP to check Illegal Migrations and Changing Demographic Distributions	@	@	@	@
15.	On Lack of population control, prevalence of polygamy among Muslims	@	@	@	@
16.	Ban on Cow Slaughter	@	@	@	@
17.	On the Muslims Education in Madarsas	@	@	@	@
18.	On the BJP's demand to check the Conversions to Islam and Christianity – Silence of Congress and other political groups	@	@	@	@

\+ Indicates the issues dealt with by the concerned author directly or implicitly.

@ Not spoken on the issue but chose to speak on other issues like banning the RSS, VHP etc. and dismissal of BJP Governments in Rajasthan, MP and Himachal Pradesh.

Table-6.11

Analysis of the Political Issues Discussed by Number of Authors – Edit Page Articles – The Hindu, Dec. 1992 -Jan. 1993

Sl. No.	Political Issues	KS
1.	Appeasement of Minorities by the Congress and other political groups	@
2.	Vote bank politics for garnering Minorities' Votes during election-Congress, Left and other Groups	@

(Contd.)

Sl. No.	*Political Issues*	*KS*
3.	Implementation of Uniform Civil Code	@
4.	Building up Consensus on disputed structures and shrines	@
5.	On the Role and Character of RSS and VHP (Communal)	@
6.	On the Communal Riots—Role of Congress (Communal)	@
7.	On the Communal Riots—Role of BJP, RSS and VHP	@
8.	On Banning Satanic Verses of Salman Rushdie-Rajiv Congress	@
9.	On Reversing Shah Bano Judgment of Supreme Court-Rajiv Congess (Vote Bank)	@
10.	On Opening the Gates of Babri Masjid-Appeasing Muslims to do prayers at Mosque—Rajiv Congress (Vote Bank)	@
11.	On Opening the Gates of Ram Lala temple appeasing Hindus and performing Shilanyas—Rajiv Congress (Vote Bank)	@
12.	On BJP 's demand for Scrapping Article 370 on Jammu and Kashmir	@
13.	On Political Alliances and Clandestine Supports from Indian Muslim League and Other Communal Bodies—Congress and other political groups	@
14.	On the demand of BJP to check Illegal Migrations and Changing Demographic Distributions	@
15.	On Lack of population control, prevalence of polygamy among Muslims	@
16.	Ban on Cow Slaughter	@
17.	On the Muslims Education in Madarasas	@
18.	On the BJP's demand to check the Conversions to Islam and Christianity—Silence of Congress and other political groups	@

@ Not spoken on the issue but chose to speak on other issues like banning the RSS, VHP etc. and dismissal of BJP Governments in Rajasthan, MP and Himachal Pradesh.

Slanted Approach

Delivering rhetoric to Hindus and Hindu Cultural Organizations on the 'secular' essence of the Hinduism, as put forward by Swami Viveknanda in his Chicago lectures without giving a similar discourse to Muslims and Muslim Cultural organizations, as if Muslims never desecrated or destroyed any Hindu temple in the post independent era marking 45 years since 1947 (The New Relevance of Vivekananda: December 30, 1992).

On Theoretical Issue What the Hindu Meant by the Term 'Secularism':

Figure 6.5 : Analysis of Scoring the Maximum Number of Authors Subscribing to the Maximum Number of Political Issues—Edit Page—The Hindu, Dec. 1992 to Jan. 1993

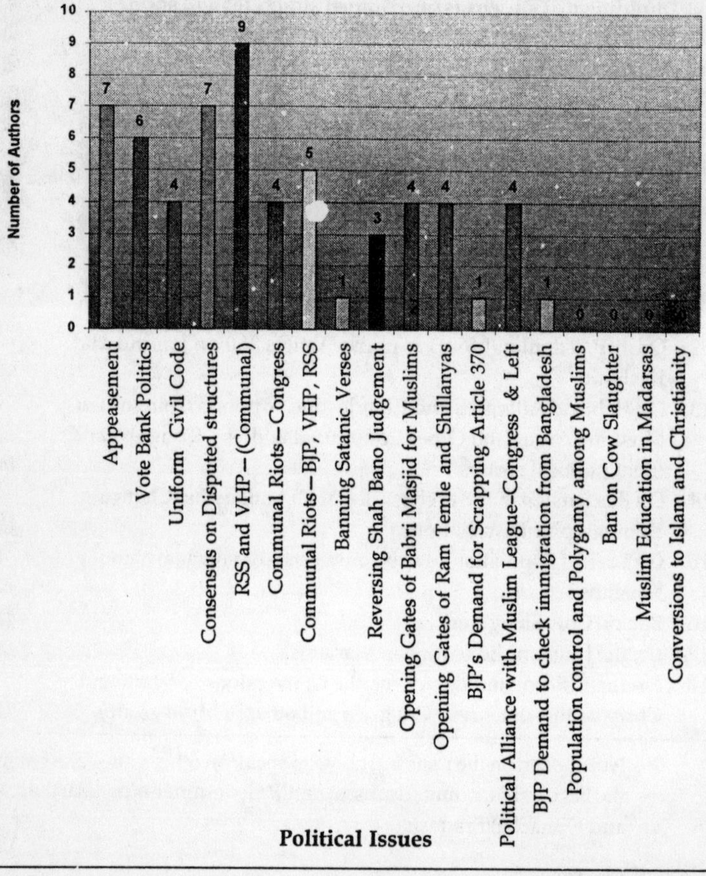

Equal treatment to all religions as the basic tenet of the brand of *secularism* ingrained in the doctrine of *secularism* in Indian Constitution (Re-establishing the Fundamental values: December 12, 1992).

From the above it would be clear the Editorial articles of the Hindu represented a clear-cut opposition to the BJP and its cultural outfits such as VHP, RSS and Bajrang Dal in so far the latter perception and philosophy of condemning the *appeasement* politics being pursued by the Congress and Left Groups. In the editorial written immediately after the demolition of Babri Masjid, 'Unforgivable' (Monday, December 7, 1992), it stated that "The shrill tenor of the Hindutva campaign, the continual jibes at *pseudo secular policies,* the inflammatory propaganda that minorities are being appeased all served to present a dangerous and false picture of Indian social reality to the public, breeding the sort of ugly fanaticism that surfaced in Ayodhya yesterday.

Though the Hindu Editorials never tried to address themselves to the theoretical or political issues raised constantly by both BJP and its cultural outfits, it seemed to have unilaterally concerned about the safety of the disputed structure and the Muslims fearing that the nation may as well embark on a course of another division similar to the partition of 1947. One can little understand such over reactions and overstatements of the problem as put out in the Editorials of the Hindu, which did not embrace itself to the full spectrum of the issue involving vital policy matters, that have been gradually alienating the majority community from other political groups, especially from Congress over decades. A statement in the editorial, 'Re-establishing the fundamental values' (December 12, 1992) goes to the extent of questioning the allowing BJP as a political entity by saying, 'Whether sectarian and communal parties ought to be allowed to bid for power under the Constitution committed to *secularism* and the equal protection of all religions is a question that needs to be pondered over." Statements such as this would skirt the much needed debate on what *secularism* meant under Indian Constitution and can *minorities* and *secularism* go together without contradiction about which a lot of criticism had already been placed in the foregoing.

Yet as a media, the Hindu should have looked into these contradictions as arising out of constitutional provisions instead of rushing to making vague statements on *secularism* purportedly that of Constitution itself. Finally its own question comes to the fore, which it has stated in its editorial, 'Re-establishing the fundamental values' (December 12, 1992), that 'Despite the current posturing, virtually all the *secular* parties now in power have been guilty at one time or the other of allying with communal parties for electoral gains'. Thus it is amply evident that the so-called *secular* parties are not indeed *secular* as much as *communal* parties not being 'communal'. As media the Hindu should have fully known that these apparent contradictions have stemmed out of improper definitions ascribed to *secularism* much to the convenience of the political establishment. Alternatively, the Hindu must have deliberately overlooked these nuances and opportunistic interpretations of *secular* parties for its own convenience in view of its strong Anti-BJP and Pro-Congress inclinations. Hence a slanted discourse could be seen in the editorial 'The New Relevance of Swami Vivekanada' (December 30, 1992). Another important feature was that in its editorials *The Hindu* indeed criticized Mr. Rao and the Congress for their lackadaisical handling of the whole issue but the critique was quite mild compared to its strong opposition to the BJP and its allies reflecting both polarization and slanting on theoretical issues. Its support to IUML and continuation of alliance with the Congress in Kerala lent further credence to this view.

Statistical Analysis

1. The Editorials of *The Hindu* showed a conspicuous and striking polarization towards Congress and displayed anti-BJP attitude in almost all, leaving its role to offer an objective assessment of the contentious issues, theoretical and political, to winds.
2. Nearly 79 per cent of the Editorials were against BJP and 7 per cent against Congress. Only 14 per cent of Editorials showed a sense of objective assessment and fair play to the contending political groups such as BJP-VHP combine.
3. Some of the Editorials were markedly slanted in their very approach and lacked in balance. Given the state of the country and the seriousness and the magnitude of the issues confronting, the Editorials would have taken the arguments of both BJP-VHP combine and Congress-Leftists groups coupled with National Front and would have given its balanced and informed decision on the merits of the issues instead of singularly accusing BJP-VHP combine indulging in communal politics.

Analysis of the Edit Page Articles in *The Hindu*

A total number of 27 articles were taken as universe of sample. It constituted contributions coming from 18 authors drawn from a variety of fields such as political parties, journalism, law and academics.

The following is the break-up of the articles to find the polarization of the paper:

1. Pro-Congress = 11 (40%)
2. Anti-BJP = 5 (19%)
3. Pro-JD = 3 (11%)
4. Anti-Congress = 1 (4%)
5. Objective = 6 (22%)
6. Pro-BJP = 1 (4%)

The percentage indicated the number of authors who discussed the issues among 18 political issues selected for the study and yet favoured a political party. It means about 11 authors, who discussed the issues raised by the BJP and yet concluded in favour of Congress, constitute 40 per cent of the total sample of study.

The following is the gist of the articles written by different authors of the universe of the sample:

Prem Shankar Jha: Pro-Congress Slanted

The author wrote six articles and all of them were aimed at criticizing the BJP-VHP combine as communal.

One often finds highly inflammable and slanted statements attributing serious motives to the BJP-VHP combined leadership. A sample of the kind of slanting could be seen from the quote given below:

Slanted Statements

1. *What is more, Mr. L.K. Advani not only endorsed the demolition of the mosque in advance but gave his tacit approval to the deed by spending the entire afternoon a bare 300 yards away, giving directions to the crowd on how to block the approach of the Central Government's security forces. He, therefore, directly precipitated the present confrontation.*
2. *You owe a deep debt of gratitude to the Congress for making all this possible. Yet, whether you are heroes or villains, nothing can alter, or redress by one jot the infinite harm that you have done to the country that you claim to revere (The choice is yours, Mr. Advani. The Hindu, January 13, 1993).*

The author is known defendant of P.V. Narasimha Rao strongly argued that P.V. was innocent of the BJP's plans to destroy the mosque that fateful day. He appreciated the immediate dismissal of Kalyan Singh government and bans imposed on the RSS, VHP etc.

Favouring P.V. Narasimha Rao, Prime Minister

By dismissing the Kalyan Singh government instead of allowing it to resign, he has called the BJP's bluff. The BJP leadership must choose between asking its three remaining governments in Madhya Pradesh, Himachal Pradesh and Gujarat to resign, and swallowing the insult and implicitly conceding that the Prime Minister's accusations are justified.

However, the author did not favor the dismissal of the BJP elected governments in the States for such a step might help consolidate the BJP's tirade against the Congress and even may make it emerge more stronger in the next round of elections where it might emerge as the sole largest opposition party (Collapse of Centrist forces, *The Hindu*, December 23, 1992).

The author however appreciated the ban imposed on the communal organizations such as RSS, VHP and Bajrang Dal. He wanted the Congress to emerge stronger in dealing with the communal groups and their demands but unfortunately the decision to allow the darshan of Ram idols at the disputed structure was allowed again which he feared might send wrong signals to the other religious groups (Can the Secular Centre revive, The Hindu, December 30, 1992; Make or break for the Congress, January 6, 1993).

Hasan Suroor—Pro JD Slanted

One article was written and it projected JD as better national political entity compared to BJP and Congress line of thinking.

The article contains highly inflammable statements against BJP-VHP combine, which instead of going into issues raised and giving a balanced treatment, prefer to accuse BJP-VHP unilaterally for all that happened.

Slanted

1. *In the ebb and flow of Hindu-Muslim relations in post-independent India, the developments in Ayodhya on Sunday represent by far*

the most vicious and regressive current no because of dilapidate, disused mosque whose exact status had in any case been disputed has been demolished but because brazen intimidation – reminiscent of fascist terror – has triumphed in full view of state machinery, if not exactly with its active connivance.

2. *For the first time, a perceived historical wrong has been 'corrected' with force deepening the sense of insecurity not only among the minorities but also the large body of Hindu secular opinion which presumably still represents the majority community and not the 'Hindu nationalist RSS' as the BBC has been saying. For, before fascism begins to devour its own children it destroys the forces of resistance – in this case, the secular Hindus who, rather than numerically and political weaker minorities, pose a greater threat to the Hindutva forces.*

Anti-Congress

1. At another level, the myopic Muslim 'leadership' fattened on non-issues and used by the Congress for its political purposes cannot escape responsibility for the rise of "Hindu Communalism.
2. By raising demands which had little bearing on Muslim 'interests' and the Government by conceding precisely such demands, they helped spread the impressions that the Muslims were being 'pampered' at the cost of the majority community' s interests, whereas the reality on the ground is that despite such 'pampering' Muslims today are the most backward community both educationally and economically; thousands have been killed in communal riots, a great language such as Urdu has been destroyed simply by identifying it with Muslims and covert discrimination in jobs has become a fact of life.

If one critically examines the above-cited points, it would be difficult to understand whether the author was in sympathy with Muslims or he was sarcastically speaking in their favour.

V.R. Krishna Iyer—Anti-BJP Slanted

One article was written and it was mainly meant to accuse BJP.

The article runs with highly emotive statements against BJP-VHP combine and in a tone of appeasement of minority community. One finds as such very slanted statements from nonetheless an eminent jurist V.R. Krishna Iyer instead of a balanced approach and judging the issues raised by the BJP-VHP combine.

Slanted

1. *Our Muslim brethren are dear and their religious sentiments must be defended by every Hindu if he is true Hindu. Patriotism has a cultural-religious dimension which transcends worship of one's own cult, sect, denomination and religion.*
2. *The vandalism has inflicted an indelible stain and incurable wound on Bharat's secular bosom.*

While using such a diatribe against BJP-VHP combine, he would innocently raise questions about the Prime Minister's reported statement that Government would rebuild the mosque at the same place and the Communists immediately demanding it. His question were whether Government can build mosques and temples claiming themselves running a *Secular* state and can Communists being agnostics demand reconstruction of mosques? "Communists *Kar Seva* for building mosques may seem bizarre."

The author seemed to have forgotten that it was precisely on this dubious credentials of the 'secular' character of Congress and Communists, the BJP-VHP combine launched the whole programme for over one decade in the name of exposing *pseudo secularism.*

P.V. Indiresan—Objective

One article was written and it was written in an objective and balanced way.

The following citations are enough to show how objectively the author approached on the subject without indulging in an emotional broadside on BJP-VHP combine:

Objective but sounds alarm on our 'secular' Constitution.

1. Babri Masjid collapsed suddenly, but the process of its destruction had a long, long gestation period. The conception and the evolution of the destructive process were rooted in certain basic defects in our socio-political structure. We need a fundamental readjustment to rectify these structural defects or else, this disaster will not end in itself instead it will be the harbinger of many more even greater catastrophes.

2. At this stage, it is very easy to condemn the BJP, the RSS and the VHP, the more important issue is why did they become as powerful as they did? Non-BJP opposition parties are trying to utilize the opportunity to settle old scores and the cut the BJP to size. In the long run, such attempts will misfire unless the problems, which the BJP espoused, are resolved.
3. The ban on communal organizations is based more on hypocrisy than on a genuine desire to do away with communalism.
4. Today every party is communal except possible to a certain extent CPI (M) and that too in Bengal only.
5. The fact is our Constitution itself is communal; the Supreme Court itself has confirmed that it is so.
6. Is not Mandal which advocates that the son of an Inspector General of Police should be preferred to the son of a poor Brahmin cook even when he has only 60 per cent marks while the Brahmin may have 80 per cent—only because his father is a Kurmi—communal?
7. If communal parties have to be abolished, Mandal also must be abolished but there is no party in India, which is prepared to take a stand against Mandal brand of communalism.
8. What our politicians are demanding is not that communalism should be abolished but only the BJP brand of communalism be abolished.
9. The Constitution enshrines certain minority rights, that is good, but it forgets that every Hindu is a minority, that is bad. Even the so-called majority communities —'Vokkaligas' or Mahrattas or Yadavas—minorities absolutely so.

The article thus has uniquely matched the criteria of objectivity laid down in the Methodology.

K.K. Katyal—Pro-Congress

The author had written 3 articles and all were Pro-Congress mostly defending P.V. Narasimha Rao for the bold steps taken by him.

Asghar Ali Engineer—Anti-BJP Slanted

The author was a known ideologue for Muslims and his entire article ran singularly criticizing the BJP-VHP combine for their alleged involvement in demolition of the structure.

Slanted

The Babri Masjid was not an ordinary mosque. It has become a symbol and the test of Indian Secularism. Its demolition shows that Indian secularism has become weak and the Congress secularism merely hollow. Rajiv Gandhi allowed shilanyas on the adjoining plot to placate the Hindutva elements and delivered a blow to secularism. Earlier he bowed down before the Muslim fundamentalists and passed the Muslim Women's Bill. Here it must be said that the Nehruvian model of secularism is the only valid model for the pluralist society of India.

Anti-BJP

Swearing by Akhandata does not make votaries of the country's unity and integrity. Those who are responsible for the demolition of the Babri Masjid cannot be champion of India's unity.

Suneet Vir Singh—Pro-JD

Total two articles were written on the kind of reporting done during the run-up to the demolition of Babri Masjid and after in The Hindu and Urdu press.

The author appeared to have a good acumen for critical reading of the press and the kind of the messages the Media is delivering during the critical time of the nation. Whereas the author was perceived a clear campaign of anti-BJP-VHP combine, The Hindi press in the hinterland of North mostly threw its weight with the BJP-VHP crusade for Ram Mandir. But some Northern Hindi-newspapers were also found to be in utter confusion as to their agenda.

Mostly the Urdu press was holding V.P. Singh as the 'symbol of secularism'. It was quite astringent against Narasimha Rao. The Newspapers Nai Dunya, Akhbare Nau of North and Rahanume Deccan and Siasat Jadeed from South – were unanimous condemning the BJP-VHP combine for demolishing the Babri Masjid. The author quoted one of the statements published in the Nai Dunya during 1989 general elections when BJP-VHP combine performed Ram Shilanyas.

"The Hindu fundamentalists, the fascist RSS and VHP and BJP, are out to destroy Babri Masjid. Stop them or else rivers of blood will flow in this country."

This is a classic example of press polarizing itself along the religious lines.

K.N. Pannikar—Anti-BJP Slanted

One article was written and it was highly slanted and prejudiced against BJP.

Pran Chopra—Pro-BJP

One article was written and it was Pro-BJP.

The author was aghast at the dismissal of three democratically elected BJP Governments apparently for no fault of them out of sheer political opportunism. It indeed was not only a wrong step of the Congress minority Government, but it once again helped consolidate BJP and VHP combine the Hindu vote banks in these states on the sympathy wave. It gave them unbridled authority to now once again focus on *pseudo secular* politics being pursued by the Congress this time with a sense of achievement of undoing some damage done to the nation by such unscrupulous politics, opined the author.

Sudhanshu Ranade—Objective

One article was written and it was purely based on objective analysis and balanced approach.

The author calls upon the Muslim brethren to realize that they cannot continue with religious bigotry like this for long as more and more they would continue to do, it would help the Hindu Majority Communalism. Rather they realize to act as Indians and its citizens first rather than as Muslims.

M.S. Prabhakara—Anti-Congress

One article was written and it criticized the Congress for its failure to live upto 'secular' character of the State.

The author says that the original desecration of the Mosque took place on December 22-23, 1949 when Ram idols were placed surreptiously inside the Mosque and an FIR was filed. It was the time when Jawaharlal Nehru was the Prime Minister and people had a lot of faith in his *secular* credentials at that time. Yet, during the time of Nehru, the idols were allowed to be worshipped not only by those who committed the act but also by the politicians who condemned it in open. Thus the very issue belonged veritably to 1949 and the present demolition of Babri Masjid was to be seen only a completion of an incomplete act due to the dubious *secular* character of Congress mainly, the author argued.

Sitaram Yechuri—Anti-BJP Slanted

One article was written and it was anti-BJP.

The article as usual of a typical Communist Politbureau Member was arrayed against BJP-VHP combine. Strangely the author, being agnostic, talks about the philosophy of Adisankara and Swami Vivekananda, as if it was to help self-flagellation of these Pro-Hindu organizations. He even quoted Bhagavad Gita preaching Sarva Dharma Samabhav.

The only unfortunate thing of all this was its unbalanced approach. Can he speak similarly to Muslims about their Islam and its importance in bringing about religious tolerance and amity with other religions?

He even failed to introspect from their party ideologies side what went wrong and how BJP-VHP combine came to have such a strangle-hold on Hindus since 1948s to 1990s.

H.R. Khanna—Objective

One article was written and it was very objective.

The article was from a legal luminary who in this article tried to state the legal position on the matters of adjudicating on the complex issues pertaining to faith and ownership of temple/land/mosque. It was an excellent erudition and exposition of how courts can indeed solve such problems.

Era Sezhiyan: Anti-BJP

One article was written and it was arrayed against BJP.

The author, in addition to his usual refrain of alleging that BJP-VHP combine indulged in belying of the Constitution, violating the Supreme Court directions, had a dig at the *kar sevaks* preventing electronic media from recording the events that led to the demolition of Babri Masjid.

Mahesh Vijapurkar: Objective

One article was written and it tried to evaluate the police role during the Bombay communal riots in the aftermath of the demolition of Babri Masjid.

The article gains insights into the heavy death toll caused during these communal riots. It clearly establishes that the heavy death toll was due to police indiscriminate firing and not because of communal riots. He called for a thorough examination of these allegations case by case though it might lead to demoralize the police force in a measure.

C.P. Bhambhri: Objective

One article was written and it was very much exposing the hollowness of our socalled 'secular' polity and political parties.

How secular are our parties?

1. How have the secular parties responded to communal politics? Every major centrist political party has operated its secularism by accommodating community interests by following the politics of vote banks. The logic of politics of vote banks had definitely harmed the goals of secularism because the secular parties made compromise with the community leaders to win the elections.
2. This compromise was dramatized by the Congress in the Shah Bano case and was further highlighted when the leaders of the *secular* parties such as the Congress I, and the Janata Dal approached the Muslim leaders for support in elections. The Shah Imam of Jama Masjid became an important luminary for the Congress I and the Janata Dal leadership. In this process, the cause of *secularism* suffered because the vote bank politics strengthened the vested interests among the communities and castes and the representatives of the communities started demanding a price from the secular parties.
3. *Secular* democracy is strengthened if the leaders of various communities have a solid base of their own and if they are able to act as authentic leaders across the communities. The Congress and the Janata Dal do not have strong community leaders whose voice is heard across the communities. The

struggle between *secularism* and communalism has become unequal because the *secular* parties are primarily concerned with strategies of winning the elections on the basis of the adjustments with the vote banks.

Kalpana Sharma—Objective

One article was written and it was regarding the communal riots in Bombay.

The article calls for an examination of police role for the escalation of communal riots.

Muchikund Dubey—Pro-Congress

One article was written and it was regarding the Bangladeshis immigration.

It was however Pro-Congress in its tone and tenor.

Statistical Analysis—(Table 5.6, Fig. 5.8)

1. As indicated earlier 11 authors out of 18 authors expressed themselves in favour of Congress, followed by 5 authors expressing strongly against BJP.
2. About 11 authors discussed the issues raised against Congress and Leftists, besides Janata Dal and National Front, and constituted 40 per cent of the universe to express in favor of Congress on all these issues. Similarly 5 authors constituted 19 per cent of the universe to express against BJP.
3. Among the contentious issues raised by the BJP, 9 authors of 18 have felt that RSS-VHP were communal. About 7 authors discussed issues of appeasement and consensus concerning the various facets of the vexed Ayodhya-Babri Masjid issue.
4. Only 4 authors strongly discussed the issues such as Uniform Civil Code, Communal Character of Congress, Opening of Temple gates for the Hindus and the Mosque Gates for the Muslims and political alliances with Muslim League, etc. and felt that these issues indeed affected the *secular* character of all the no-BJP political parties, especially Congress and National Front.
5. As many as 6 authors indulged in making highly emotional and imbalanced statements smacked of blatant slanting and

deviation from the balanced approach. The slanting has been distinctly identified as opposing the BJP or Congress or JD or National Front, etc. Those statements have been highlighted with italicized paragraphs in the respective author's content analysis. In fact, only a few important 'slanted' statements have been highlighted here though there are many more in each of the articles of those authors.

Analysis of Non-Edit Page Articles

There were 5 articles of reporting which were selected as a sample of the universe corresponding to the period. Some of them were bureau reporting whereas one was a straight write-up from Prem Shankar Jha.

These were examined on the basis of the selected political issues in order for arriving at a quick comparison with those content that was reflected in Editorials and Edit Page articles to determine whether thc News bureau reporting of the Hindu differed with that of the other content in material, polarization and facts.

The following break-up gives the ideal polarization of the reportage of these clippings:

1. Anti-BJP = 4
2. Objective = 1

The following analysis of these articles would give the further insight into the subject treated for the study.

Rewriting History—The BJP Way: Anti-BJP Slanted*

The very first sentence of the introduction sounds like either slanting or sensationalizing the educational policy of the BJP ruled States including Uttar Pradesh and Madhya Pradesh.

**Slanted*

1. *A major and systematic effort is afoot in two BJP ruled States—Uttar Pradesh and Madhya Pradesh—to reorient the study of history. The idea is to bring about far-reaching pro-Hindutva changes in the curricula prescribed in schools and colleges as well as creating parallel boards to conduct examinations, especially in schools run by the Sangh Parivar.*

The entire statement was apparently not based on any material evidence or any statement of the Government at the Ministerial level. It was only a conjecture and it even meant that the State Governments duly elected by the people on a different political mandate were not competent enough to contemplate any changes that would look appropriate to their political ideologies.

While the write-up hints at large scale revision of the curricula, the example it cites in the same report is 3-line change in the history text prescribed for Classes 9 and 10 in Uttar Pradesh, which reads:

2. *Babur's Commander Mir Baqi constructed a mosque on the spot where a temple was destroyed. Even though this structure is under dispute, the Hindus consider this structure a temple even today.*

It would not be clear what was the biggest change achieved favouring Hindutva in the inclusion of the above statement. It was a historical fact that Babri Masjid was constructed by Mir Baqi. It was also a fact that many Hindus believe that it was the birthplace of Ram. It was also a fact that a dispute regarding this existed since the time of British and after independence it started getting hot. In other words the present Government of UP wanted to introduce existence of this controversy to students of next generation in a very soft and mellowed away. Didn't an elected State Government have the right to tell its subjects on the basis of which it verily came to power?

Similarly a few such slanted statements were reproduced here how the reporting was smacked of anti-BJP.

3. *.......even though the Aryans are said to have migrated from Central Asia, 'recent research in this area is increasingly establishing the hypothesis that Aryans were the original inhabitants of India.*

4. *Similarly, the history texts in these States will conform to the principle of recalling the glorious traditions of the medieval chieftains such as Maharana Pratap Singh and Shivaji. However, presenting Akbar and Aurangazeb as victors over their Indian contemporaries will only belittle the tradition of India in the minds of young students.*

Interesting Finds from Debris, Say Experts: Anti-BJP Slanted

It is another news clipping that appeared in The Hindu which gloat over the VHP failure to provide a clinching and conclusive evidence that a Ram Temple was destroyed to give way to a Masjid.

The article began reporting that the VHP produced another piece of evidence suggestive of existence of a temple at the place where mosque was built citing the archaeological evidence. At the same time, it would make a derisive laugh at the VHP that the Muslim leaders of the Babri Masjid Action Committee contested these findings and produced alternative evidence to counter the VHP's claims.

The following paragraph establishes the sarcasm unleashed at VHP and its claims:

Slanted

When that theory was countered by independent experts brought in by the All India Babri Masjid Action Committee, digging and levelling by the PWE men around the complex unearthed some 'new' and 'amazing' finds around June/July this year and displayed by the VHP at Ayodhya and submitted as evidence during the talks held by the Narasimha Rao Government. Once more the VHP claimed that 'conclusive evidence' had been found of an ancient temple. However, they had found a Shiva statue and could not explain what that was doing in a Ram temple.

Vajpayee Calls for Equality of Religions: Objective

It was an article written fairly reporting the lecture delivered by Atal Behari Vajpayee in the Dr. Rajendra Prasad Memorial Lectures Organized by All India Radio, Bhopal.

A sample of objective reporting could be gauged without attributing motives or calling pot shots at his speech was given below:

Objective

Nonetheless, his lengthy prepared text, a scholarly treatise on 'Secularism: The Indian Concept" was a treat to the discerning mind.

It was a Countdown for a Fascist Coup: Anti-BJP Slanted

The report was sent by the Special Correspondent even as the talks were progressing between the Government and the contending rival groups, VHP and AIBMAC (All India Babri Masjid Action Committee).

The report however was very speculative of ominous developments in its opening sentence the 'intro' that reads like this:

Slanted

> *As the Ayodhya talks progressed, it became clear to the Government that not a Ram Temple at Ayodhya, but the 'overthrow' of a democratic secular Constitution to establish a fascist, Hindu theological state was the clear objective of the Sangh Parivar.*

The above sentence was a classic example of how to write a slanted intro for report without any basic or justification even to arrive at such statements.

The article after the 'intro' appeared to be a summing up of whole issue in retrospect tracing down the talks between VHP and AIBMAC since October 3, 1992 to October 23, 1992 after which the talks did not proceed ahead for obvious reasons. But the report seemed to be fingering VHP rather than AIBMAC though not substantiated.

Prem Shankar Jha: Crucial Days for the Nation: Anti-BJP

The article was written in the non-Edit pages by the writer Prem Shanker Jha, who was press information secretary to P.V. Narasimha Rao that time.

The article was written within two days after the demolition of Babri Masjid. It was anti-BJP in its treatment.

However, some of the statements of the write-up are really worth pondering over.

1. The greatest danger that Indian democracy faces today is therefore not from the Hindu fundamentalists but from the over-reaction of the *secularists*.
2. The National Front-Left may not be doing it consciously, but they are playing an old and familiar game. This is to combine with the far right to bring down the Centre. The more they push the Government into harsh and undiscriminating

action against the Sangh Parivar, the more will they confer on it the halo of martyrdom, incense ordinary Hindus and make them flock to its banner.

3. In the same way all those who must have been in the conspiracy to bring down the mosque or have blatantly instigated it, like Ashok Singhal, Uma Bharati and Rithambara Devi and even Advani, whose insistence that the Garbha Griha would be where the mosque now stood, played no small part in legitimizing the destruction need to be arrested.
4. But the past experiences have shown that bans on communal organizations invariably increase their appeal.

Analysis of Sunday Magazine Articles

One article, 'We have met the enemy, and he is us' written by Madhu Limaye was taken as universe since it covered all aspects of the events in the run upto the Demolition of Babri Masjid. It was an exhaustive article published with photographs of destruction of Babri Masjid spread over 3 to 4 pages of The Hindu Sunday Magazine, dated December 13, 1992.

Another article communalism: A view from the South' was also taken for its value of analysis on the link between economic development and religious bigotry among Muslims in the South and North. It was also an exhaustive article that was based on author and eminent journalist, Saeed Naqvi's recent book 'Reflections of an Indian Muslim' (The author reviews his own book here in this article).

It may also be mentioned here that in the study conducted, the subsequent articles that appeared in Sunday Magazine on this subject were not so exhaustive as were covered by the two above and as to the content contained almost same information without adding any new dimensions that had been already discussed in various other forms in the Hindu.

Both the articles were oriented to anti-BJP treatment.

Madhu Limaye : We Have Met the Enemy, He is Us: Anti-BJP

The author tried to trace the statements of the leaders of BJP, especially Advani since the time of making firm commitment to abide by the Constitution and then going to the people to the day of making a statement 'that it was unfortunate that the structure was demolished'.

Some of the examples are given here to know how biased the statements were.

Anti-BJP-VHP

1. "It is now clear that all these statements and assurances were in the nature of camouflage, a big hoax, a dirty confidence trick. It now appears that the entire Sangh Parivar and the Kalyan Singh Government were privy to the plan of the demolition of the structure. The howl raised against the deployment of Central forces by the BJP and the inaction of the PAC posted 'near' the disputed structure, the affidavit before the Supreme Court, the flood of reassuring statements and assurances were all part of gigantic fraud."
2. "To me this is not a surprise. I have been familiar with the RSS Parivar tactics these last fifty-five years. The Parivar believes in the doctrine of 'The End Justifies The Means'. They are votaries of Machiavellianism. They glorify this and call it 'Krishnaneeti."
3. But the BJP leaders are all puppets. They were never leaders of an autonomous party. They are mere instruments of the RSS. It is the RSS which is at the root of this tragedy.

Favouring Congress and P.V. Narasimha Rao

"Was P.V. Narasimha Rao, then wrong in pursuing the method of conciliation? I do not think so. After all, as the election results of 1990 showed, a considerable section of our electorate has been communalized thanks to the poisonous propaganda carried on for over a decade, the mistake of the previous Congress and non-Congress Governments, both in Lucknow and Delhi, the inept handling of the explosive issue by V.P. Singh (we must remember how he issued an Ordinance acquiring the disputed land and then repealed it within 24 hours and that his chief preoccupation was his factional feud with Chief Minister Mulayam Singh), and above all, the peculiar parliamentary situation created by the electoral verdict. It was therefore necessary to make the utmost effort to find a compromise solution. The Prime Minister was not wrong in exploring avenues of peaceful settlement.

Communalism: A View from the South: Objective

The approach of the author looked quite novel. Like many academics, he tried to look at economic angle and religious bigotry and fanaticism among Muslims.

Objective

1. Muslims in the South are different from their Northern brethren, though not quite as different as, say, Persina Muslims (the world's largest Muslim population resides in Indonesia) and those in Saudi Arabia, all the bogus talk of the durability of a pan-Islamic link notwithstanding. The more oppressed a community, the greater the tendency to fall back on its larger myths; the more economically disadvantaged a Muslim, the greater his inclination to trace direct descent from Akbar the Great. This invites reaction from the majority community. Not that this alone caused riots. But it certainly conditioned the temperature between two communities.
2. None of this nonsense in the South. The Labbals or the Tamil speaking Muslims, who settled on the east coast largely in districts like Kanyakumari, Tirunelveli and Ramana-thapuram are today among the more prooperous in the State, controlling among the dubious black market in South-East Asia. Similarly, the Navayats who spread out from the Konkan and Kerala coasts are thriving businessmen. The per capita income of Muslims in Karnataka is higher than that of their counterparts up in North.
3. The Muslims in the South did not come as conquerors; they came as traders. It would hardly have been good business to go about proselytizing. They identified themselves totally with the language and culture of the area of their trade. Not only do they speak the regional language, but have produced literature in these languages. I am told one of the better known authorities of Kamba Ramayana is Justice Ismail. As for music Chinna Maulana Sahib, the great nadaswaram player, playing in total devotion to Hindu gods.
4. But compared to South, the situation in North was different. There the Muslims were not traders. Conversions and Minority complex linked to religious bigotry appeared to have sent the waves of backlash by Hindus.

Analysis of Interviews

These interviews were given by eminent politicians in the aftermath of the demolition of the Babri Masjid. Mr. Arjun Singh, Mr. Harkishen Singh Surjeet, Mr. Chandrasekhar, Mr. V.P. Singh and Mr. Vajpayee interviews had been taken as sample universe for they discussed on all issues selected for the study.

As expected their arguments in the interviews which they had given on the lines of their political ideology least admitting their own fallacies in so far their contribution to the meaning of the term 'secularism'.

Arjun Singh: (Congress Leader): Anti-BJP

1. A known opponent of BJP, accuses the latter for acting in a manner that is above the interests of the nation.
2. Strongly supports dismissal of BJP State Governments and imposition of ban of RSS, VHP and Bajrang Dal.
3. Doesn't introspect regarding the popular criticism about the *secular* credentials of the Congress.

Harikishen Singh Surjeet : (Communist Party Marxist Leader): Anti-BJP

1. Surjeet calls for a unification of all *secular* forces to fight against *communal* forces obviously BJP-VHP combine.
2. Doesn't introspect whether their *secular* credentials are fool-proof.
3. Supports the dismissal of BJP State Governments in MP, HP and Rajasthan.

Chandrasekhar: (Former Prime Minister of India): Anti-BJP

1. Alleges the failure of the Congress Government for not taking a firm line on the Ayodhya issue and entertaining a dialogue and conciliatory approach.
2. Says that majority of Indians are not with the BJP.
3. Does not agree for any punitive steps against BJP-VHP combine or the BJP ruled States.

V.P. Singh (Former Prime Minister of India): Anti-BJP

1. Admits that the parties were busy in the Centre in making and unmaking the Governments.

2. Admits that Mandal and Minority issues raked by his Government sent signals to BJP and its combine to usher in different brand of politics which led to the demolition of Babri Masjid and consequent communal clashes across the country.
3. Also admits the other than political polarizations, corruption and erosion of values in public life also contributed to the deterioration and sliding of the country.

Vajpayee (the Leader of the BJP): Pro-BJP

1. Admits that the demolition of Babri Masjid was a grave mistake but refuted any preplanned conspiracy.
2. Opposes the ban on VHP, RSS and Bajrang Dal.
3. Opposes the dismissal of the State Governments in MP, HP and Rajasthan.
4. Traces the events to the *pseudo secular policies* pursued by the Congress, Left and National Front leaders.
5. Says that BJP's path is true *secular* and not what is defined as *secular* in the Constitution.
6. Refutes the allegations of 'historical revenge', 'communal', etc.

7

Discussion and Conclusions

As discussed in the Chapter 1 the media role over years got intricately linked to the evolution of Politics and the Polity of a nation, especially in democratic countries like India where media is accorded the status of fourth estate. As such media trends also have been undergoing severe changes, its primary role to act objectively notwithstanding. The present study is meant to focus on, as outlined in the objectives of the study and in the hypothesis, whether there is any change in its basic responsibility to perform its role objectively while dealing with issues of sensitive and far reaching one such as the current subject of hot debate like the character of *secularism* sought to be pursued under the framework of Constitution and the brand of *secularism* being followed by the political parties governing the nation both at the Centre and the States. What follows is a discussion centering round this basic premise.

Usually, to begin with, Editorials are considered as the mandate of the Managements of the Newspapers. They broadly reflect the line of thinking of the concerned management running the Newspaper. Therefore, the discussion on the analysis given already in earlier Chapters 5 and 6 would begin with the Editorials of the two leading National Newspapers.

Treatment of Editorials of the *Indian Express* and *The Hindu*

Emphasis: More in Indian Express

As stated earlier the emphasis on the subject of the study *secularism*, viewed from the prism of 'Ayodyha' and 'Babri Masjid' or 'majorityism' and 'minorityism', was quite high in the Editorials of the Indian Express compared to the Editorials of The Hindu. Between December 4, 1992 to January 8, 1993 about 26 Editorials appeared on this subject straight or on the allied subject in Indian Express as against 13 Editorials appeared in The Hindu during the same period (Tables 5.1 and 5.7).

Political Alignment: Indian Express Pro-BJP and The Hindu Pro-Congress

Out of the 26 Editorials written on the subject in Indian Express about 12 Editorials (46%) were supportive of BJP either directly or in the nature of supporting the issues raked up by the BJP-VHP-RSS combine. On the other hand, out of 13 Editorials written on the subject in The Hindu about 11 (79%) articles were either directly against BJP or in the nature of opposing the issued raised by the BJP-VHP-RSS combine (Figures 5.1 and 5.7).

Whereas Indian Express wrote 8 Editorials (31%) against the Congress on various acts of commission and omission on the issues of Ayodhya and on arriving at a consensus with the rival parties, including its own dubious *secular* credentials, The Hindu during the same period wrote only one anti-Congress Editorial (7%). In fact The Hindu was much appreciative of the Congress and its leadership for the stringent steps – imposing ban on RSS, VHP and dismissal of the elected BJP Governments in the States of Madhya Pradesh, Himachal Pradesh and Rajasthan – it had taken in the aftermath of the demolition of the Babri Masjid.

Objectivity: More in Indian Express, Less in The Hindu

As for the objective role, which both the giants of the Press are bound to show, only 6 Editorials (23%) appeared in the Indian Express compared to 2 Editorials (14%) written in The Hindu were very objective and advisory in nature, showing a sense of balance both in the emotion and the content. Even by this reckoning it appeared Indian Express displayed more concern on the issues dogging the nation than The Hindu (Figures 5.1 and 5.7).

Slanted: The Hindu

Whereas the treatment of the content in Indian Express inclined towards BJP-VHP combine, it was issue based not holistic. There was no effort in these Editorials to justify the actions of these institutions, which included the demolition of Babri Masjid, the grand culmination of all actions of these organizations thus far they had done to support their ideology. At the same time there was no effort to teach the Hindus the significance of religious tolerance; nor did they (Editorials) try to teach Muslims. The articles were balanced. But the Editorials of The Hindu at times tried to teach the Hindus the greatness of the Hindu religion whereas not a single word was written advising Muslims also to maintain religious harmony. It appeared that the maintenance of *secular* values was solely the Hindus' responsibility in which Muslims had no part in India (The New Relevance of Vivekananda, December 30, 1992).

Polarization

From the above it would be clear that the two Newspapers at a crucial time in the history of nation since independence had taken diametrically opposite views and stand on a very controversial, yet of far reaching consequences, subject 'secularism' along the sidelines of aligning themselves with the two major political parties, Congress and the BJP.

Agreement on Theoretical Issues: Indian Express for BJP-VHP line of 'Secularism"; The Hindu Vague

The Editorials of the Indian Express did not subscribe to the present import of the term 'secularism' in Indian Constitution brought in under 42 amendment by late Mrs. Indira Gandhi. On other it appeared to have aligned with the BJP-VHP combine's line of argument that the present import of the term *secularism* is discriminatory and pro-minority, especially encouraging appeasement and vote bank politics. It was more in favor of the term 'secularism' which means equality of all religions without any pro-minority trappings. Contrary to this stated position of Indian Express, most of the Editorials of The Hindu appeared to be vague on this most sensitive and vexed issue. Some Editorials agreed with the present import of the term *secularism* with all its underpinnings to Minorities as defined in the Constitution. At the same time in some Editorials The Hindu too advocated the equality of all religions without the pro-minority inclinations (Table 6.4).

Agreement on Political Issues

Concerning the 18 political issues, which were selected for the study for detailed analysis and treatment of the same by Editorials, the present study found that the Indian Express Editorials have agreed 8 important issues as contentious having affected the *secular* character of India and its political parties, and did not speak at all on 10 other issues (Table 6.7). On the contrary, The Hindu Editorials have agreed that only 4 important issues as contentious and disagreed with as many as 5 issues. Nearly 9 issues remained untouched by The Hindu Editorials (Table 6.7 and Figure 6.5).

Treatment of Edit Page Articles of *Indian Express* and *The Hindu*

Emphasis: More in The Hindu

Indian Express published Edit Page 23 articles on the subject of *secularism* and the Ayodhya movement, which consequently led to the demolition of Babri Masjid, between December 3, 1992 and January 8, 1993. Eminent journalists, ideologues and political science experts wrote the articles on this subject. On the other, The Hindu published about 27 articles on the subject in its Edit Page contributed by similar category of writers (Tables 5.2 and 5.9).

Of the 23 articles written in Indian Express, 7 (29%) articles were in favour of BJP either directly or through the issues raised by the BJP against the 'secular' credentials of other political groups. On the side of The Hindu 11(40%) articles were in favor of Congress either directly or through the issues raised by the BJP as contentious (Figures 5.9 and 5.10).

When it came to content analysis, an interesting observation stemmed out of the critical reading of the above articles. Whereas Pro-BJP and Pro-Congress treatment of articles could remain so without any complication of interpretation, the anti-Congress articles appearing both in the Indian Express and The Hindu agreed directly or indirectly with the line of thinking of BJP-VHP combine on the issues raised for the study. That way anti-Congress articles or their content would add upto the BJP-VHP lot. Thus in the case of Indian Express the Pro-BJP and Anti-Congress articles would add up to 12 (50%) articles (See Table 5.2 and Figure 5.3). Similarly in The Hindu, the Pro-BJP article 1 (4%) together with anti-Congress article 1(4%) would add up to total 2 articles directly or indirectly agreeing with the BJP line of thinking on the contentious issues raised. Conversely the 5 Anti-BJP articles (19%) too would add up to the Pro-Congress either directly or indirectly on the issues raised (See Figure 5.8).

Political Alignment: Indian Express Pro-BJP and The Hindu Pro-Congress

In short based on the above analysis of emphasis it would be clear that the Indian Express authors favourably disposed (50%) in favor of the contentious issues that the BJP raised as much as the authors who disposed in favor of the Congress (63%) in *The Hindu*.

Objectivity: Indian Express and The Hindu at Same Level

In the case of Indian Express about 4 (17%) articles were absolutely objective and two (8%) were purely theoretical. In total 6 articles (25%) of Indian Express, which dealt with the contentious issues based on the merits and demerits of the respective schools of thought were equal to the number objective articles (6) in The Hindu.

Slanted: The Hindu Allowed More Slanting in the Articles than the Indian Express

Out of 23 articles selected for the study from Indian Express 4 articles were identified (See Chapter 5) as slanted against the issues raised by the BJP-VHP Combine articles, where 6 articles in The Hindu were identified as heavily slanted against BJP-VHP (See Chapter 6).

Polarization

From the above discussion it would be obvious that both the Indian Express and The Hindu showed signs of political polarization even in regard to publishing the articles in its Edit Page by different authors. In a surprise encounter the author of the study encountered two excellent articles of Suneet Vir Singh who quoted the reporting of the Hindi Press and the Urdu Press on the developments of Ayodhya. The author showed by quoting the paragraphs of Hindi Press and the Urdu Press, how the Press got polarized itself along the political lines in India during this period (Urdu Press on Ayodhya, December 16, 1992; Confusion in the Hindi Press, December 17, 1992).

Agreeing on Political Issues: (Indian Express Highlighted More Issues than The Hindu).

Out of 18 political issues, identified for the present study, which were contentious and affecting the *secular* character of the country and the political parties, about 10 authors (10 out of 16 authors) who wrote articles to the Edit Page of Indian Express agreed that 5 issues were indeed contentious and affected the *secular* fabric of the country. On the contrary 9 authors out of 18 who wrote to The Hindu agreed that one issue, the RSS-VHP being communal, affecting the *secular* character of the Country and political parties. Similarly 7 authors out of 18 agreed that two issues, appeasement and consensus on the disputed structure, as contentious and affecting the *secular* stature of the Indian polity.

Treatment of Non-Edit Page Articles in *Indian Express* and *The Hindu*

The Non-Edit Page articles constitute articles written by different personalities hailing from Politics, Law, Journalism and other fields, and published in News Paper anywhere such as front page as anchor item or shoulder item or inner page article other than Edit page. Especially in the aftermath of the demolition of Babri Masjid, Indian Express ran a special column called Counter Point for a week or more. Articles published in the Counter Point were also included in this in view of the significance of the subject and relevance to the time.

About 15 articles of such category were selected as universe of the study from Non-Edit pages of Indian Express between December 18, 1992 to January 4, 1993. Fourteen authors contributed these articles (Table 5.3). On the other hand, there were no such articles except News Bureau Reports or reports of the anonymous Special Correspondents in The Hindu during the corresponding period. From among those 5 articles relevant for the study were taken as the universe (Table 5.7).

Emphasis: More in Indian Express

Out of the 15 articles contributed by 14 authors hailing from the fields like Politics, Journalism, Law and religious bodies, 7 articles (46%) were treated for Pro-BJP-VHP combine on the political issues which they raised as contentious and affecting the *secular* fabric of the country (Table 5.3, Figure 5.3). About 5 articles (33%) were written against BJP-VHP combine as to the contentious Political issues raised by them. One article was written for anti-Cong (7%). Based on the earlier logic that the articles related to anti-Cong in principle agreed on the contentious issues raised by the BJP-VHP combine as affecting the secular fabric, the total treatment in favor of BJP-VHP combine would rise to 53 per cent (7+1=8 articles). On the other out of 5 articles in The Hindu, 4 articles (80%) were written against BJP-VHP combine's contentious issues and one article (20%) was written very objectively with a balanced approach and emotional appeal (Figure 6.1).

Political Alignment: Indian Express Pro-BJP and The Hindu Anti-BJP

As observed in the case of Edit Page articles, in respect of Non-Edit Page articles also, the Indian Express apparently gave more patronage to the articles which reflected the views of the BJP-VHP combine on the contentious issues compared to The Hindu which in keeping with its pattern in the Edit Page articles patronized anti-BJP-VHP articles which opposed the views of these political and cultural organizations on the contentious issues.

Objectivity: Both Indian Express and The Hindu at same level

Out of 15 articles published in the Non-Edit Page of Indian Express only one article appeared to be very balanced on the issues raised as contentious by the BJP-VHP combine on the *secular* polity of India since independence. Similarly out of 5 articles in The Hindu only one appeared to be very objective giving a balanced consideration. However, the 'objective' role of the both papers was at stake from the foregoing.

Slanted The Hindu Allowed More Slanting than Indian Express

Out of 15 articles published in the Non-Edit Pages of Indian Express, 4 articles were slanted whereas 5 articles of Non-Edit Page published in The Hindu 3 articles were slanted. Compared to the very less number of articles (5) taken for the study from The Hindu, 3 articles writing in a slanted way is certainly very high as against 4 out of 15 of Indian Express.

Polarization: Indian Express Pro-BJP; The Hindu Pro-Congress

Both the reputed national level dailies strikingly shown their political inclinations or subscription to the ideas reflected by the BJP or the Congress.

Scoring on Political Issues

The 15 articles appeared in the Non-Edit Pages of Indian Express were evaluated for their agreeing on the contentious political issues. Out of 14 authors 11 authors agreed that two issues, Appeasement and Vote Bank Politics, were indeed contentious issues affecting the 'secular' character of the nation. About 8 authors opined that two issues, opening the gates of Babri Masjid for Muslims and temple for the Hindus, had changed the *secular* character of the Government as well as Congress Party.

On the other, the articles published in The Hindu did not agree with any of these issues and hence opposed the BJP-VHP combine tooth and nail. As a result the 'slanting' in The Hindu articles was found to be very high reflecting the unilateral treatment of the subject.

Treatment of Articles Published in Sunday Magazine of *Indian Express* and *The Hindu*

Total 7 articles published between November 9, 1992 to January 3, 1993 from the Indian Express for the were taken for the study as universe. Similarly two articles published in *The Hindu* between December 6 to December 13, 1992 were taken for the study. The reason for a small selection of the sample was not author's choice. In fact both the Indian Express and The Hindu did not publish any major articles beyond these days in their Sunday Magazines. Their priorities shifted on some other topics such as banning the cultural organizations such as VHP, RSS and Bajrang Dal and dismissal of the BJP State Governments, communal riots, etc. As such, the articles which covered the theoretical and political issues were limited to these few articles published in the Sunday Magazines of the Indian Express and The Hindu respectively.

Further, the sample of the Sunday Magazines of Indian Express and The Hindu did not in fact constitute any new trend than what had already been established in respect of the Editorials, Edit Page

Articles and Non-Edit Page articles. Thus the present sample quantitatively would not add any difference to what had been already analyzed. In view of the small quantity of the sample, the author did not take bargraphs or pie charts for the analysis. Simple treatment analysis was carried out just to find out whether they differed from the findings of the foregoing in any distinct way that warrant a more detailed study from the other dimensions and additional samples.

Emphasis: More in Indian Express

In the total 7 articles written in the Sunday Magazine of the Indian Express, 3 articles were written by Talveen Singh who was a regular columnist. Of the remaining 4 one was a book review by M.M. Shankdher and one was by the News Bureau's report compiled by Bhaskar Roy and his team. Out of the left over two articles one was written by Rejee Suri and another was by Goutam Sen.

All articles were written against BJP-VHP combine's contentious issues. Especially Talveen Singh wrote 3 weeks consecutively on the same issue yet she concluded that the arguments of BJP-VHP combine drifting to 'fascism'. Likewise all the others had chosen one direction or the other to attack BJP-VHP combine.

On the other The Hindu published two articles in its Sunday Magazine. Whereas one was written very objectively on the contentious issues raised by the BJP-VHP combine by Saeed Naqvi, the other was written by Madhu Limaye the Socialist leader known for his credentials to oppose BJP-VHP combine ideologically for long. Thus compared to Indian Express, the emphasis in the Hindu was quite less.

It also appeared that the Indian Express purposely tried to treat the articles it published in its Sunday Magazine in the trend quite opposed to its pursued trend on the regular days. Alternatively it could be an error due to the very small sample from both the Indian Express and The Hindu.

Political Alignment: Both Indian Express and The Hindu Looked Anti-BJP

Out of 7 articles published in Indian Express all were arrayed against BJP-VHP combine's contentious issues. Similarly the 2 articles published in The Hindu were also aimed at accusing the BJP-VHP.

Objectivity: Both Indian Express and The Hindu are Less Objective

Whereas not a single article was objective out of 7 articles published in the Sunday Magazine of Indian Express was objective, one of the two articles published in The Hindu written by Saeed Naqvi was indeed balanced and offered a new angle and some interesting insights on some of the issues raised by the BJP-VHP combine. It also explained partly why Indian Express subscribed to the ideological contentions of the BJP-VHP as opposed to The Hindu.

Slanted

None of the articles published in Sunday Magazines of the Indian Express or The Hindu was found to be slanted.

Polarization: More Anti-BJP

The articles published in both the Sunday Magazines of Indian Express and the Hindu were clearly showing anti-BJP inclinations. As such this may be an error due to the size of the small sample.

Interviews Published in *The Hindu*

Though the author included this as sample for the study, there was no parallel publication of similar interviews in the Indian Express during the same period. Further important political leaders that time, including two former Prime Ministers gave these interviews which went in accordance with their political schools of thought. As such the author is not willing to take this as a reasonable sample of consequence for comparison and to draw any conclusions on the basis of it as it may lead to unexpected errors in the so far scientifically analyzed discussion.

Conclusions

1. The study as analyzed and discussed in the foregoing, clearly established that there was vagueness surrounding the term *secularism* and *secular character* of the nation, constitution and political parties with regard to both theoretical issues and political issues.
2. Confusion over the actual import of the term *secular* existed

even among the Editorials written by the Editors of both the Indian Express and The Hindu. Neither the Indian Express Editorials nor the Editorials of The Hindu attempted to discuss what is the true meaning and understanding of the word 'secular' appropriate to Indian context.

3. At this time when nation as a whole is caught up in communal flames and engaged in headlong discussions over the appropriate meaning to the term 'secularism', neither the Indian Express nor the Hindu offered to give a direction and guidance to the society by way of offering a range of meanings applicable to the Indian context.
4. Nor did they engage the authors, contributors, journalists towards giving such a guidance to the populace of India in general (Social Responsibility Theory).
5. On the other they published unrestricted views of the authors who, barring a few, again indulged in routine rhetoric and popular arguments in keeping their schools of thought, ideology and political affiliations such as Leftist leanings or Pro-BJP leanings or Pro-Congress leanings.
6. As such the role of Gatekeeping and acting as a *Watchdog* – both of which the Media could have offered to the vast readership went seriously missing and wanting.
7. *Gatekeeping* could at best have been done in the given context by subjecting the articles of authors, journalists, academicians and politicians to a balanced or meaningful presentation of ideas offering a comprehensive issue to the readers rather than onesided approach of the writers in the content. It would have enhanced the credibility and readability of the Newspapers.
8. For instance while publishing the Editorial or Edit Page or non-Edit Page articles, it could have better read and identified whether the particular write up subscribe to *Sarvadharma Samabhav* or *Dharma Nirapekshata* as far as 'secularism' pursued in India by the political groups is concerned. Such an exercise would have enhanced the clarity of the content free from confusion. To achieve such a clarity, the Media could have developed a format into which the views expressed by the authors should be have been built or fitted.
9. Instead of publishing scathing comments filled with such powerful vocabulary as 'fascists' 'barbaric', 'nazis', the

Newspaper could have established some norms of conveying messages without subjecting the audience to the same level of aggressiveness with which the content was written by the writers.

10. A plethora of terminology came into existence during this crucial period: Fundamentalism, Communalism, Positive Secularism, Revivalism, Culturualism, Fascism, Nazism, Pseudo-secularism without an appropriate definition or meaning in the context of India.
11. It clearly proved the hypothesis of this dissertation that the media lost its basic function of *objectivity* to be achieved through *watchdogicsm and gatekeeping* and aligned itself to specific contentions of political and cultural organizations.
12. Compared to The Hindu, Indian Express gave more coverage and canvass for serious discussion on the contentious issues as raised by the BJP-VHP combine.
13. Whereas Indian Express gave more weight to the issues by involving writers from various walks to arouse popular opinion among the people, The Hindu had taken one sided approach and almost allowed articles, both in Edit and Non-Edit Pages, that toed similar line of thinking.

Suggestions for Further Study

The author recommends further study on the subject with a larger sample from different dimensions to determine whether the media exhibited similar polarization on the lines of political ideologies both prior to and after the demolition.

Bibliography

Adishanakara: *The Commentary on Upanishads:* Ramakrishna Mutt Publications, Calcutta, 1998.

Amrik Singh: Congress in a Fix: The Out Manoeuvred Party has to Reorient its Ideology. *Indian Express Edit Page*, January 1, 1993.

Amrita Abraham: Neither Hindu virtue nor Constitutional Propriety. Indian Express Edit Page, January 8, 1993.

Arjun Singh: We should be firm in dealing with Communal Elements: Arjun Singh, *The Hindu,* December 11, 1992.

Arun Nehru: Appeasement Policy has proved bane of the Nation, *Indian Express*, January 3, 1993.

Arun Patnaik and K.S.R.V.S. Chalam: *The Ideology and Politics of Hindutva in the Region, Religion, Caste, Gender and Culture in Contemporary India.* Ed. TV Satya Murthy. Oxford University Press, Vol 3, pp. 252-280, 1996.

Asghar Ali Engineer: "Introduction" to Saral Jhingran's Secularism in India: A Reappraisal, Har Anand Publications, New Delhi, p. 12, 1995.

Asghar Ali Engineer (ed): *Religion and Liberalism,* Ajanta Publications. Delhi, 1989.

Asghar Ali Engineer: Tampering with History: Hinduising Textbooks will Cause Alienation, *Indian Express Edit Page*, December 8, 1992.

Asghar Ali Engineer: Test for secular forces. *The Hindu Edit Page,* December 15, 1992.

Asghar Ali Engineer: "Hindu-Muslim Relations Before and After 1947 in Anatomy of Confrontation. *The Babri Masjid-Ramajanmabhoomi issue,* Ed. S.Gopal. Penguin Books India (P) Ltd. pp. 179-192, 1993.

Atal Behari Vajpayee: BJP not for a Communal Divide. *The Hindu,* December 1992.

Avijit Pathak: The Ayodhya Tragedy: Collapse of Reason, Faith and Secularism, *Indian Express Edit Page*, December 23, 1992.

Berelson, B., *Content Analysis in Communication Research*, New York, The Free Press, 18, 1952.

Bharat Bhushan: Choice Before Congress: Straight Fight Against Communalism or Becoming BJP's-B Team, *Indian Express Edit Page*. December 25, 1992.

Bharat Bhushan: Unable to Lead: Mr. Rao has Failed both the Nation and the Congress. *Indian Express Edit Page*. December 11, 1992.

Bhasker Roy: Out Laws Again. *Indian Express Spotlight*, December 20, 1992.

Bhambhri, C.P: Ayodhya and the Indian State, *The Hindu Edit Page*, December 29, 1992.

Bilgrami Akeel: Two Concepts of Secularism: Reason, Modernity and Archmedean Ideal, *Economic and Political Weekly*, July 9, 1994, pp. 1749-1761.

Boenhoeffer, D.: *Letters and Papers from Prison*, 7th Imp. London Collins Fontana 1965, (New Edition London SCM Press 1971).

Bruce, S. (ed): Religion and Modernization. *Sociologists and Historians. Debate the Secularization Thesis*. Oxford. Claredon Press,1992.

Budd, S. (ed): *Sociology and Religion*, New York, Macmillan. 1991.

Budd, S: *Varieties of Unbelief: Atheists and Agnostics in English Society*. 1850-1960, London, Heinemann, 1977.

Callahan, D. (ed): *The Secular Society Debate*, London, Collier Macmillan. 1966.

Chalapathi, Rau: 200 Years of the Indian Press, *Vidura*, February, 1980.

Chatterjee, Partha: *Secularism and Toleration: Economic and Political Weekly*, July 9, 1994, pp. 1768-1777.

Clarke, P.B. and Linzey, A. (ed): *Dictionary of Ethics, Theology and Society*. Routledge, London and NY, p. 747, 1997.

Cox, H: The Secular City: *Secularization and Urbanization in Theological Perspective*, London SCM, 1969.

Deutschmann, P.J.: *Newspaper Content of Twelve Metropolitan Dailies, Cincinnati*, Scrips-Howard Research, pp. 92-95, 1959.

Dharma Kumar: *Left Secularists and Communalism. Econnomic and Political Weekly*, July 9, pp. 1803-1809, 1994.

Dobbelaere, K.: Secularization – A Multidimensional Concept, Current Sociology, Vol. 28 (2). p.5, 1981.

Durga Das Basu: *An Introduction to Constitution of India* (15th edition). Prentice Hall, New Delhi, pp. 26-29: 1993.

Era Sezhiyan: Disservice to Press Freedom: *The Hindu Edit Page*, December 24, 1992.

Finke, R. and Stark, R: The Churching of America 1776-1990. Winners and Losers in our Religious Economy, New Brunshwick, NJ, Rutger University Press, US, 1992.

Fowler, J.W.: *Stages of Faith: The Psychology of Human Development* and the Quest for Meaning. Harper and Row, Sanfrancisco, 1981.

Gautam Sen: Hindu Pride is no Sin, *Indian Express*, November 29, 1992.

Gopal, S: *Introduction to Anatomy of a Confrontation – The Babri Masjid-Ramajanmabhoomi* (ed) S.Gopal, Penguin Books India (P)Ltd. New Delhi, pp. 11-21, 1993.

Goswami, N.: A Carnival of Clones, *Indian Express*, New Delhi, July 24, 1994.

Greeley, A.M.: *The Persistence of Religion*, London, SCM, 1973.

Gunaratne,S: Media Subservience and Developmental Journalism. Communication and Development Review, Vol. 2, No. 2, pp. 3-7, 1996.

H.R. Khanna: The Role of the Courts, *The Hindu Edit Page*, December 22, 1992.

Hanumantha Rao Ch: Religious Fundamentalism: The Challenge has to be Met with People's Involvement, *Indian Express Edit Page*, 1993.

Harkishen Singh Surjeet: Joint Front Should Involve All Secular Forces. *The Hindu*, December 18, 1992.

Hasan Suroor: A Noble Dream Shattered, *The Hindu Edit Page*, December 9, 1992.

Hiranmay Karlekar: The Shredded Consensus: The Disastrous Implications of Further Polarization. *Indian Express Edit Page*, December 26, 1992.

Hiranmay Karlekar: Exorcising Comunalism: The need to define a new Philosophy of Freedom, *Indian Express Edit Page*, December 12, 1992.

Holyoake, G.J.: *Secularism: The Practical Philosophy of the People*. Holyoake GJ & Co., London, 1854.

Holsti, O.: *Content Analysis for the Social Sciences and Humanities,* Reading, MA. Addision-Wesley, pp. 167-94, 1969.

Irfan Habib: *The Case for Reason: Arguing with Communalism.* January 5, 1993.

J. Swaminathan: Shades of Nazism, *Indian Express,* January 4, 1993.

Jagmohan: Crisis of the Polity: Need for a Pervasive Reform Movement. *Indian Express Edit Page,* January 5, 1993.

Janis, I.L. and Fadener, R.: The Coefficient of Imbalance. in H.D. Laswell *et al.* Ed. *The Language of Politics: A Quantitative Semantics,* Cambridge, MIT, pp. 55-82, 1965.

John, R. Hinnells (ed): *A New Dictionary of Religion.* Black Well Publishers Ltd., London, p. 458. 1995.

Kamat, H.V.: C.A.D. Vol. VII, pp. 831-33 quoted in Saral Jhingran's *Secularism in India*: A Reappraisal, Har Anand Publications, p. 57, 1995.

K. Govinda Kutty: Left Logic: Then and Now. *Indian Express,* December 21, 1992.

K.K. Katyal: Clear Lines, Unclear Future, *The Hindu Edit Page,* December 21. 1992.

K.K. Katyal: The Parties After the Trauma, *The Hindu Edit Page,* December 14, 1992.

K.K. Katyal: December 6 and after, *The Hindu Edit Page,* January 4, 1993.

K.K. Katyal: Varied Response to Ayodhya, *The Hindu Edit Page,* January 1, 1993.

K.N. Panikkar: The Task Before the Nation, *The Hindu Edit Page,* December 16, 1992.

K.R. Malkani: Misuse of History: Pakistan's Diet of Falsehood for the Young, *Indian Express Edit Page,* 1992.

K.R. Malkani: Significance of Ayodhya: Working out the Indic Thesis, Antithesis and Synthesis, *Indian Express Edit Page,* 1992.

K.S. Duggal: The Frenzied Fringe, *Indian Express,* January 4, 1993.

Kalpana Sharma: Why were Bombay Riots So Fierce? *The Hindu Edit Page,* December 29, 1992.

Krishna Mahajan: High Court uses Rama's Sketch to define Secularism, January 12, 1993.

Laswell, H. Nathan Leites and Associates: *The Language of Politics*, Cambridge, Massachusettes. MIT Press, 1965.

L.K. Advani: Arjun Singh Played Mulayam this time, *Indian Express*, December 18, 1992.

L.K. Advani: The BJP is Unequivocally Committed to Secularism, *Indian Express*, December 27, 1992.

Lesley Brown (ed): *The New Shorter Oxford English Dictionary on Historical Principles*, Vol. 2, No. 2, Oxford-Claredon Press, London, p. 2753, 1933.

Madan, T.N.: Secularism in Its Place. Delivered as a Lecture on the Occasion of the 1987 Meeting of the Association of Asian Studies in Boston, and Published in the *Journal of Asian Studies*, Vol. 46, pp. 747-759. November, 1987.

Maheswari, S.R: Abuse of Article 356: President's Rule has been Imposed 86 times, *Indian Express Edit Page*, December 22, 1992.

M.M. Sankhdher: Glimpses of Spicy Journalese. A Review on 'Reflections of an Indian Muslim' of Saeed Naqvi (Har-Anand Publications) *Indian Express*, December 6, 1992.

M.M. Shankdher: The Solution Lies with the Muslims, *Indian Express*, January 2, 1993.

M.S. Prabhakara: Can Cong (I) Keep Its Promises, *The Hindu Edit Page*, December 21, 1992.

Madhu Limaye: We Have Met the Enemy, and He is Us, The Hindu Sunday Magazine, December 13, 1992.

Martin, D.A.: *General Theory of Secularization*, Oxford Blackwell, 1978.

Mahesh Vijapurkar: Police and the Bombay Riots: *The Hindu Edit Page*, December 24,1992.

Mohan Dharia: Ayodhya Tragedy and After: Need for a Patriotic Approach to Fight Communal Forces, *Indian Express Edit Page*, December 28, 1992.

Muchikund Dubey: Inept Handling of a Sensitive Issue, *The Hindu Edit Page*, 1993.

Murthy, D.V.R.: *Developmental News Coverage in the Indian Press: Media Asia*, Vol No. 27, No.i, 2000.

Mushirul Hasan: Competing Symbols and Shared Codes: Inter-Community Relations in Modern India in Anatory of a Confrontation: *Babri Masjid-Ram Janmabhoomi Issue*, Ed. S.Gopal, pp. 99-121, 1993.

Mushirul Hasan: The Changing Position of the Muslims and the Political Future of Secularism in India in *The Region, Religion, Caste, Gender and Culture in Contemporary India*. Ed. T.V. Satya Murthy. Oxford University Press. Vol. 3, pp. 200-228, 1996.

Nagamallika, G.: *The Coverage of Communal Riots in the Hyderabad based Daily Newspapers*, Ph.D Thesis, Univ of Hyderabad, 2002.

Nasir Tyabji: *Political Economy of Secularism: Rediscovery of India, Economic and Political Weekly*, July 9, pp. 1798-1801, 1994.

Nawab Zafar Jung: Healing the Wounds, *Indian Express*, January 4, 1993.

Niraja Gopal Jayal: *The State and Democracy in India or What happened to Welfare, Secularism and Development in Niraja Gopal Jayal Ed. Democracy in India*, Oxford University Press, New Delhi, pp. 193-224, 2001.

Noorani, A.G.: *Legal Aspects to the Issue in Anatomy of a Confrontation: The Babri Masjid-Ramjanmabhoomi Issue*. Ed. S.Gopal. Penguin Books India (P) Ltd., New Delhi, pp. 58-98. 1993.

P. Parameswaran: Why Ayodhya is Crucial for the Nation? *Indian Express*, January 9, 1993.

Philip Bab Cock Gove and Merriam Webster Edit Staff (ed): *Webster's Third New International Dictionary*. Merriam Webster Inc. USA. p. 2053, 1993.

P.V. Indiresan: Ayodhya and Structural Adjustment: *The Hindu Edit Page*, December 12, 1992.

Pran Chopra: Ayodhya and Macro Politics, *The Hindu Edit Page*, December 19, 1992.

Prem Shankar Jha: Can the Secular Centre Revive? *The Hindu Edit Page*, December 30, 1992.

Prem Shankar Jha: Collapse of Centrist Forces, *The Hindu Edit Page*, December 23, 1992.

Prem Shankar Jha: Crucial Days for the Nation, *The Hindu*, December 9, 1992.

Prem Shankar Jha: Make or Break for the Congress, *The Hindu Edit Page*, 1993.

Prem Shankar Jha: The Beginning of a Long War, *The Hindu Edit Page*, December 17, 1992.

Prem Shankar Jha: The BJP's Hour of Reckoning, *The Hindu Edit Page*, December 8, 1992.

Prem Shankar Jha: The Choice is yours, Mr. Advani, *The Hindu Edit Page*, January 13, 1993.

R.L. M. Patil: Secularism: The Fall of a False God, *Indian Express*, December 19, 1992.

Radhakrishnan S.: "Foreword" to S.Abid Hussain's *The National Culture of India*, pp. vii-viii. 1956.

Rajagopalachari: Quoted in D.E. Smith's *India as a Secular State*, p. 151. 1963.

Rajeev Bhargava: Giving Secularism its Due, *Economic and Political Weekly*, July 9, pp. 1784-1791, 1994.

Rajee Suri: *Shrines in the Shadows: Sunday Magazine, Indian Express*, January 3, 1993.

Rajni Kothari: The Hindutva Philosophy: Contradictions within the Ayodhya Movement, Indian Express Edit Page, January 21, 1993.

Roy, M.N.: India's Message, Ajanta Publications, Delhi, 1982.

Saeed Naqvi: Communalism: A View from the South, *The Hindu Sunday Magazine*, December 6, 1992.

Salman Khursheed: How Does One Repair a Damaged Hinduism? Indian Express, January 2, 1993.

Saral Jhingran: *Secularism in India: A Reappraisal*. Har-Anand Publications, New Delhi, p. 53, 1995.

Shah, A.B.: Religion and Society in India, *Indian Secular Society*, Pune, 1981.

Shiner, L.: The Concept of Secularization in Empirical Research. *Journal for the Scientific Study of Religions*, Vol. 6 (2), pp. 207-220, 1967.

Signorielli N., McLeod, D. & Helay, E: Gender Stereotypes in MTV Commercials, Journal of Broadcasting and Electronoic Media, 38(1), pp. 91-101, 1994.

Sinha, V.K.: *Secularism in India*, Lalwani, Bombay, 1968.

Sitaram Yechuri: Fascistic Pseudo-Hinduism: *The Hindu Edit Page*, December 22, 1992.

Smith, D.E.: *India as a Secular State. New Jersey*: Princeton University Press, US, 1963.

Soli Sorabjee: Outrageous Onslaught on the Constitution, *Indian Express*, January, 1993.

Sudipta Kaviraj: *Religion, Politics and Modernity:* (Chapter 14) in Crisis and Change in Contemporary India, (Eds) Upendra Baxi and Bikhru Parekh, pp. 249-316, 1995.

Sujata Patel: *On the Discourse of Communalism in The Region, Religion, Caste, Gender and Culture in Contemporary India,* Ed. T.V. Satya Murthy, Oxford University Press, Vol. 3, pp. 144-176, 1996.

Sri Nirvikalpananda Swami: *Commentary on Bhagavadgita.* Ramakrishna Mutt, Calcutta, 1966.

Stempel, G. H. III: *Content Analysis in Stempl III GH and Wesley BH Research Methods in Mass Communication,* Englewood Cliffs. NJ, Prentice Hall, pp. 119-131. 1989.

Sudhanshu Ranade: Can We Swim or Must be Sink: *The Hindu Edit Page,* December 19, 1992.

Suneet Vir Singh: Confusion in the Hindu Press: *The Hindu Edit Page,* December 17, 1992.

Suneet Vir Singh: Urdu Press on Ayodhya, *The Hindu Edit Page,* December 16, 1992.

Swami Vivekananda: *Karma Yoga, Bhakti Yoga, Gnana Yoga and Raja Yoga,* Ramakrishna Mutt Publications, Calcutta, 1989.

Swami Vivekananda: *Complete Works.* Ramakrishna Mutt Publications, Calcutta, 1989.

Swapan Dasgupta: Metaphorically, We are All Kar Sevaks Now, *Indian Express,* January 4, 1993.

Talveen Singh: Regain the Initiative, *Indian Express,* December 27, 1992.

Talveen Singh: The Pseudo-fascists, *Indian Express,* November 11, 1992.

Talveen Singh: The Saffron Scourge, *Indian Express,* December 13, 1992.

Telang G.M.: The BJP's Chance: Imperatives of Power Pursuits in a Democracy, *Indian Express Edit Page,* December 3, 1992.

Telang, G.M.: BJP at Cross-Roads, Restoring Sense of Proportion in Righting Religious Wrongs. *Indian Express Edit Page,* December 31, 1992.

Vanaik, A.: Spectre of Hindu Rashtra: Secular Forces must Unite to Face Decisive Challenge, *Indian Express Edit Page,* December 19, 1992.

Vanaik, A.: The Parivar Project: Creating Hatred to Mould Hindu Unity. *Indian Express Edit Page,* January 4, 1993.

Vanaik, A.: Situating Threat of Hindu Nationalism: Problems with Fascist Paradigm, *Economic and Political Weekly,* July 9, pp. 1929-1743, 1994.

Venkata Subba Rao, G.C:*Indian Constitutional Law,* Vol. II, Commentaries, C. Subba Chetty & Co., Madras., pp. 525-32.

Virendra Kapoor: Ram Temple Inevitable, Rao Can Find a Solution Now to Avert a Conflagration Later. *Indian Express Edit Page,* December 10, 1992.

Virendra Kapoor: Aftermath of December 6 From Census to Confrontation Could Prove Suicidal, *Indian Express Edit Page,* December 10, 1992.

Virendra Kapoor: Heritage Against Harmony: Time for Muslims to Reassess Their Role in Society, *Indian Express Edit Page,* January 7, 1993.

Vilanilam, J.V.: *Mass Communication in India: A Sociological Perspective.* Sage Publications, New Delhi, 2005.

V.P. Singh: Hindu Militancy Will Lead to Bloodshed: *The Hindu,* December 28, 1992.

V.R. Krishna Iyer: A Barbarity and Otiosity: *The Hindu Edit Page,* December 10, 1992.

Wimmer, R.D. and Dominick J.R: *Mass Media Research: An Introduction,* 7th Edition, Thomson-Wadsworth, pp. 139-163. 2003.

Wilson, B.R.: *Religion in Sociological Perspective,* Oxford University Press, London, 1982.

Index

Abraham, Amrita 60, 65, 91
Absolute Truth 33
Acclaimed Authors 20
Adi Shankara 32-34, 46
Advani, L.K. 58, 79, 81-82, 85, 88, 92-94, 99, 106, 119, 133
Affiliations 110
- Political 65, 148
- Religious 38-39

Afghan Warlords 83
Aggression 80
Agnosticism 28, 32
Agreement on
- Political Issues 141
- Theoretical Issues 140

Ambdekar, B.R. 39-40
Analysis
- of Agreement and Disagreement 109
- of Articles of Sunday Magazine 99
- of Interviews 136
- of Non-Edit
  - Page Articles 129
  - Page Articles Written 92
- Political 52
- of Political Issues Discussed 65, 67-69, 71, 73-75

Ancient Hindu Temples 19
Ancient Temples 19, 131
Andhra Pradesh 23
ANOVA 11, 22
Anti-BJP 55, 60, 62, 64, 79, 87, 98-101, 103-06, 108, 119, 124, 126, 129, 132-33, 136
Anti-Congress 56, 58, 83-84, 87-88, 90-91, 93, 97, 102, 104, 119, 121, 125
Anti-Religionism 3
Appeasement 52, 57, 94-97, 99, 101, 121, 128, 140, 143
- and Vote Bank Politics 145
- Blatant 93
- Brazen 80
- of Minorities 17, 65, 67-69, 71, 73-75, 109, 111-14
- of Minorities 6, 99
- Policy 62
- Political 93
- Politics 92, 94, 116

Arab World 83
Article Communalism 133
Articles
- Anti-Congress 141
- Patronized Anti-BJP-VHP 144
- in Sunday Magazine 20-21

Atheism 32, 36
Atom Bomb 3
Aurangazeb 130
Authors
- Marches 80
- Hailing 143

Ayodhya 3, 45, 47, 49, 51, 53, 59, 62, 80-82, 84, 93, 97-98, 106, 117, 131-32
- Dispute 76

Lethal Weapons 19
Movement 141
Temple 48

Babri Masjid 3, 8, 9, 23-24, 49-52, 55, 58-59, 82-83, 85-86, 91-94, 97-99, 102-04, 124, 126-28, 132-33, 136-41
Action Committee 131-32
Demolition of 3, 8, 23-24, 46, 51-52, 55, 58-59, 82, 85-86, 93-94, 99, 102, 126-27, 137, 140-41
Destroy 124
Disputed 17
Gates of 92, 145
in Ayodhya 48
-Ramjanmabhoomi 51
Structure 83
Bajrang Dal 19, 58, 102-03, 116, 137, 145
Basu, Durga Das 1, 3, 36, 38
BBC 121
Benaras Hindu University 89
Bhagavad Gita 32-33, 46
Bhambhri, C.P. 106, 127
Bhargava, Rajeev 44-45
Bilgrami, Akeel 45-46
BJP-Governments 110, 112, 114-45
Dismissal of 66, 68-70, 72, 74-76, 109, 113
Role of 17, 66-67, 68-69, 72, 73-74, 76, 110-13, 115
-VHP 146
Bombay Communal Riots 106, 127
Bosnian Muslims 83
Brahman 32-33
British Colonialism 42
Brown, Lesley 25
Buddhism 4, 33
Bukhari, Shahi Imam Abdulla 18

Cabinet Committee on Political Affairs 50-51
Campaign 82
Launching Election 50
Started Election 51
Chandrasekhar 136
Chatterjee, Partha 45
Check Illegal Migrations 66-67, 69, 70, 72, 111, 113-15
Christianity 28, 112-15
Church 3-4, 25-26, 29, 30, 35, 37, 41
Coefficient of Correlation 22
Cold War 28
Communal
Amity 86
Bodies 66-67, 69-70, 73, 75-76, 111, 113-15
Character 6, 8
Clashes 137
Crisis 44
Elements 6, 108
Forces 136
Harmony 60
Neutrality 78
Riots 12, 17, 66-69, 72-76, 111-13, 115, 121, 127-28, 145
Role of BJP 110
Role of Congress 67, 109
Communalism 41-43, 60, 62, 84-85, 108, 123, 128, 134, 149
Discourse of 43
Communications and Development Review 12
Communist Party Marxist Leader 136
Communist Politbureau Member 126
Communists Kar Seva 122
Congress
and National Front 93, 128
Bharat Bhushan 60
Government 17, 97, 136
in Kerala Lent 118
-Leftists Groups 118
Minority Government 125
-Ruled States 58

Secularism 124
Silence of 66, 68-69, 70, 72, 74, 75, 110, 112-15
Congressmen 97
Consciousness
Perpetuate Communal 39
Religious 44
Constitution
of India 3-4
and Supreme Court 17
Constitutional Canvass 8
Content Analysis 8, 10, 18, 21-22, 48, 129, 141
Continuance of Benaras Hindu University and Aligarh Muslim University 89
Conversions
and Christianity 66, 68-70, 72, 74-76, 112-15
of Low Caste Hindus 18
To Islam
Cow Slaughter 18, 40, 66-67, 69-70, 72-73, 75-76, 110-11, 113-15
Crisis
and Change in Contemporary India 44
Unprecedented Political 10

Da Vanci Code 45
Darshan 53, 95, 103-04, 120
Threat 56
Tickets 40
Deccan Chronicle 23
Delhi University 42
Demographic Distributions 67, 69, 70, 72-73, 75-76, 110-11, 113-15
Desai, Morarji 5-6
Directive Principles of State Policy 17, 39-40
Dirty Confidence Trick 134
Disturbing Implications 103-04

Edit Page 62, 64, 141-42, 145, 148
Articles 144
of Indian Express 143
Editorial
Remarks 104
Anti-Congress 139
Editors of Indian Express 20
Ekam Sat Vipra Bahuda Vadanti 34
Election
Campaigns 49
Manifesto 49
Electronic Media 1
Preventing 126
Elements, Secular-Progressive 82
Emergency 2, 4-5, 88
Engineer, Asghar Ali 37-38, 47, 65, 87, 92, 123
English Newspapers 23
Ethics of Media 11

Failure of Congress 58

Gandhi, Indira 4
Gandhi, Rajiv 50, 85-86, 124
Gupta, Swapan Das 50, 62

Hasan, Mushirul 43, 51-52, 86
Hindi Press 106, 124, 142
Hindu
and Hindu Temples 19
and Muslims in India 88
Communalism 121
Communalists 85
Editorials 117, 141
Fundamentalists 124, 132
Grievance 86
Majority Communalism, 125
Nationalism 45, 80
Threat of 45
Sentiments 86
Temples 19
Vote Banks 17, 125
Hinduism 34, 42, 46, 49, 62, 83, 96, 106, 115
Hindutva 44, 60, 83, 88, 90, 94, 96, 117, 121, 124, 129-30

Campaign 117
Elements 124
Forces 121
Party 83
Hosti Formula for Reliability 21

Illustrated Weekly of India 53
Indian Constitution for Scheduled Castes 39
Indian Contemporaries 130
Indian Culture 88, 96
Indian Democracy 132
Indian Express 2, 8-9, 16, 20, 23-24, 47, 51, 53, 55, 58-65, 67-69, 71, 73-75, 94, 99, 109, 138-49
Sunday Magazine of 145, 147
Indian Fascism 79
Indian Media 55
Indian Secularism 49, 124
Inflammable Statements 120
International Red Cross 83
Interviews 54, 136, 147
Islam 4, 18, 34-35, 41-42, 47, 66, 68-70, 72, 74-76, 80-81, 83, 94, 96, 98, 110, 112-15, 126
and Christianity 18, 34-35, 66, 68-70, 72-76, 110, 112-14
Islamic
Nations 20
Religion 19
Sevak Sangh 85
Somalia 83
World 83
ISS 85
IUML 104, 118

Jainism 33, 35
Jammu and Kashmir 18, 66-67, 69-70, 72-73, 75-76, 88-89, 92, 110-11, 113-14
Janata Dal 47, 51-52, 54, 88, 101, 104, 127-28
Jawaharlal Nehru University 42
Jha, Prem Shankar 105-07, 129, 132
Joshi, Murali Manohar 58
Journalism 65, 143
Jung, Nawab Zafar 93

Kalyan Singh Government 58, 134
Kar Seva 53, 103, 126
in Ayodhya on December 59
Kar Sevaks 19
King, Martin Luther 35
Kumar, Dharma 42

Lal, Devi 93
Latin Secularis 25
Left Secularists 42
Leftists 44, 85, 93-94, 97, 118, 128
Lickert Scales 11
Limaye, Madhu 108, 133, 146
Lok Dal 47
Lok Sabha 5-6, 52
Lord Krishna 32-33
Lord Ram 52-53, 82-83, 95-96
Low Caste Hindus 18
Lucknow Division Bench of Allahabad High Court 52

Machiavellianism 134
Maharana Pratap Singh 130
Mandal 52, 93, 123, 137
and Minority Issues 137
Brand of Communalism 123
Card 52
Combination 52
Mandalism 88
Masjids 19, 48-49, 53
Mass Communication in India 1
Mass Media Research 13
Mathura 19, 48-49, 53
Media
Analyses 9
Asia 12
Institutions 10
Subservience and Developmental Journalism 12
Trends 138

Minorities 3-8, 34, 36-38, 45, 59, 80, 84, 96-97, 99, 117, 121-23
 Intolerance 45
 Communalism 100
Minorityism 88, 94-95, 138
Monotheistic Faiths 35
Muslim
 Bodies 95
 Communalists 85
 Fearing 117
 Girls 94
 Identity Consciousness 43
 League 18, 66-67, 69-70, 72-73, 75-76, 89, 104, 110-11, 113-15, 128
 Organizations 19, 52, 78, 81, 86
 Populations 18
 Reformers 95

Naqvi, Saeed 100, 108, 133, 146-47
Narayan, Jayaprakash 2, 5, 49
National Agenda 82
National Front 54, 92-94, 97, 118, 128-29, 132, 137
Nazism, Shades of 62
Nehru, Arun 51-52, 93
Nehru, Jawaharlal 5, 17, 39, 42-43, 46, 51-52, 61-62, 87-88, 93, 125
News
 Bureau Reports 143
 Clipping 131
Non-Edit
 Page Articles 143-44, 146
 Pages of Indian Express 143
North Muslims 100
Nuisance Value 2
Nyaaya Visehika 32

Opportunistic Alliances 18

Panth Nirapekshata 47
Pathak, Avijit 65, 86
Political
 Establishment 118
 Issues 16-17, 65-76, 109-15, 141, 143
 Opportunism 125
Positive Secularism 17, 149
Press Statements and Contributions 16, 18, 20
Privatization 30
Pro-BJP
 and Anti-Congress Articles 141
 and Pro-Congress Treatment of Articles 141
 Leanings 148
 -VHP 143
Pro-Congress 60, 102-04, 118-19, 123, 128, 139, 142, 145, 148
Progressive-Secular Tango 82
Pro-Minority Inclinations 140
Pro-Muslim 87, 104
Pseudo-Hinduism 79
Punjabi Muslims in Pakistan 83

Rajendra Prasad Memorial Lecture 47, 78, 131
Rallying Point 9, 54
Ram Temple 49, 60, 77, 92-93, 95-96, 99, 131-32
 Gates 92
Ramjanma Bhoomi 54, 85
Rao, Narasimha 51, 59, 81-85, 103, 120, 123-24, 131-32, 134
 and Congress 59, 83
Rashtriya Swayam Sevak Sangh 19, 102-03, 116, 137, 145
 Nature of 17
 Role and Character of 66-69, 72-75, 109, 111-13, 115
Rath Yatra 45, 91
Rationalization 27, 29, 31
Rau, Chalapati 1
Reddy, Sanjeeva 6
Rediscovery of India 43
Reforms 40, 92

Religious
  Agencies 30
  Agents 27
Relocate 79, 90-91
Rishis 32-34
Roy, Bhasker 99-100
Rushdie, Salman 50

Sampling 15
Satanic Verses, Banning of 17, 92
Schools of Philosophy 33-34
Scoring on Political Issues 145
Secular
  Activities 30
  Agencies 29
  Center 106, 120
  Character 6, 36-37, 39, 50-54, 64, 92, 126, 141, 143, 145, 147
  Control 27
  Country 89, 91
  Credentials 47, 59, 104, 125, 136, 139
  Culture 31
  Forces 93, 108, 136
  Identities 44
  Issues 91
  Life 46
  Model of Indian Constitution 17
  Parties 117-18, 127-28
  State 36-39, 42, 79
  Stature 143
Secularism 3-11, 18, 23-29, 32-33, 36-39, 41-47, 49, 52, 54-55, 58-60, 64, 79, 81, 88-89, 91, 93, 96-101, 116-18, 122, 124, 127-28, 136, 138, 140-41, 147-49
Secularists 45, 53, 132
Secularity 26-27, 35, 39, 79
Secularization 26-31, 34-35, 38
Shah Bano Case 17, 40, 51, 86, 95, 127
Shah Imam of Jama Masjid 127
Shariat Law 18
Shastri, Lal Bahadur 5, 81
Shiv Sena 47
Shiva Shrine 35
Singh National Democratic 104
Singh, Amrik 65, 90
Singh, Arjun 82, 136
Singh, Choudhury Charan 6
Singh, Kalyan 58, 103, 120, 134
Singh, Talveen 99, 101, 146
Singh, V.P. 51, 108
Singhal, Ashok 133
Slanted Statements 78-80, 92, 94, 96, 98, 119, 122, 130
Sociology of Religions 26
Soonyavaada 32
State Socialism 3
Sunday Magazines 16, 145, 147
Supreme Court 17, 40, 50-51, 59, 70, 74, 76, 78, 86, 95, 103, 110-11, 123, 126, 134
Swami Vivekananda 33, 41, 46, 115, 126
  New Relevance of 104, 115, 118, 140

T- Test 11
Television Coverage of Presidential Campaign 15
Temple
  Administration 40
  Cleanliness 40
  Claiming 122
Thematic Analysis and Theoretical Issues 11
Theologians 28
Theoretical
  Issues of Secularism 17
  Statements 85
Third New International Dictionary 26
Third World Democratic Countries 2

Tolerance 19-20, 34, 48, 83, 96, 126, 140
Treatment of
Edit Page Articles of Indian Express 141
Editorials 104, 138
Non-Edit Page Articles in Indian Express 143
Press Statements and Special Contributions 62, 107
Treaty of Westphalia 27
Tyabji, Nasir 43

Uma Bharati and Rithambara Devi 133
Uniform Civil Code 17, 39, 128
Implementation of 66-69, 72-75, 109, 111-13, 115
United Nations 88
University of Hyderabad 12
Urdu Press 106, 124, 142
on Ayodhya 142
Uttar Pradesh 50, 103, 129-30

Vajpayee, Atal Behari 5, 47, 78-79, 107-08, 131, 136-37
Vanaik, Achin 45, 65, 79, 92
Vijapurkar, Mahesh 106, 127
Viswa Hindu Parishad 17-19, 22, 46-47, 49, 53, 58-59, 61, 66-70, 72-78, 82, 84-87, 93-103, 109-16, 118-26, 128, 131-32, 134, 136-37, 139-47, 149
Role and Character of 66-69, 72-75, 109, 111-13, 115
Vivekananda Kendra 53
Vote Bank 66-68, 70, 72-74, 76, 110-12, 114-15, 145
and Appeasement 99
Politics 17, 66-69, 71, 73-75, 92, 109, 111-14

Western Concept of Religion 34
Western Model of Content 11-12
Western Secular Model 17, 109
Winds Pitching 11
Write-up 129-30, 132

Yadavas 123
Yechuri, Sitaram 126
Yogeswara 32